PENGUIN BOOKS

THE NATIONAL TRUST MANUAL OF HOUSEKEEPING

Hermione Sandwith has a degree in the history of art from London University. In the aftermath of the Florence floods of 1966 she had two years' valuable experience of the practical conservation of works of art at the Uffizi in Florence and at the Istituto del Restauro in Rome. She joined the National Trust in 1974 and has played a leading part in setting up the Trust's Conservation Service. She is now Deputy to the Surveyor of Conservation with special responsibility for paintings.

Sheila Stainton trained as an occupation therapist. She has a long-standing interest in the conservation of textiles and spent three years helping to establish the Textile Conservation Centre at Hampton Court. She has worked for the National Trust since 1961 on textile repairs and in 1977 was appointed the Trust's first Housekeeper. In this capacity she travels extensively, giving advice on the maintenance of proper conservation standards in the houses in the care of the Trust.

THE
NATIONAL TRUST
MANUAL OF HOUSEKEEPING

Compiled by
HERMIONE SANDWITH
and
SHEILA STAINTON

PENGUIN BOOKS
in association with the
NATIONAL TRUST

Penguin Books Ltd, Harmondsworth, Middlesex, England
Viking Penguin Inc., 40 West 23rd Street, New York, New York 10010, U.S.A.
Penguin Books Australia Ltd, Ringwood, Victoria, Australia
Penguin Books Canada Ltd, 2801 John Street, Markham, Ontario, Canada L3R 1B4
Penguin Books (N.Z.) Ltd, 182–190 Wairau Road, Auckland 10, New Zealand

First published by Allen Lane Ltd in association with The National Trust 1984
Published in Penguin Books 1985

Made and printed in Great Britain by
Butler & Tanner Ltd, Frome and London

CONTENTS

What we have delivered in this Treatise, we took
not upon Trust or Hearsay, but by our own per-
sonal knowledge and experience do promise and
aver, that if you punctually observe them, you
must of necessity succeed well; and if any Gentle-
men or Ladies, having met with disappointments
in some of the Receipts, do question the truth and
reality of them, they may for their satisfaction (if
it stands with their convenience) see them tried
by the Auther, according to the very rules set
down . . .

Stalker and Parker,
A Treatise of Japanning and Varnishing, 1688

1. The servants at Erddig in 1912, carrying the implements of their occupations

FOREWORD

BY DAVID WINFIELD

Surveyor of Conservation to the National Trust

The housekeeper of a country house was concerned with the day-to-day upkeep of its contents, as well as the supervision of the female staff and the comfort of the owner and his family. The historic buildings representatives and house staff of the National Trust, for whom this Manual was first compiled, are concerned with the preservation of the Trust's possessions for ever.

These two words 'for ever' are simple enough to say, and even though the task they imply is impossible to achieve, they must never be forgotten, underlining as they do the difference between the housekeeper of old who was concerned only with maintenance and our far greater task today.

The purpose of maintenance is to preserve in good working order. Most of us spend some of our time in this way. We see that the car is serviced; we wash and mend clothes; we paint and decorate the house. In maintaining we are helping to preserve our possessions.

The National Trust's responsibility for preservation is different and ever-lasting, and that is why the Housekeeping Manual came into being. It is the first publication to bridge the gap between the old maintenance and modern conservation. We have called it a 'Housekeeping' rather than a 'Conservation' Manual, because good housekeeping is part of what we would call preventive conservation, and the Manual is for those who 'housekeep' or look after things rather than for the professional conservator. Our aim is to ensure that as few objects as possible decline to the point where they need repair. Neither accident nor *Anno Domini* can be avoided, and since all things begin to decay from the moment they are made, conservation treatment will be necessary over the years at more or less regular intervals. Nevertheless the skills of the conservator would be of no use without the continuing care taken by the 'housekeepers' – in a National Trust house, the staff.

The most difficult task is to maintain the right environment. It is a matter of compromising, of finding levels of temperature and humidity, for example, which will suit the woodwork, although it would prefer to be more damp, and at the same time keeping paper happy, even though it would like to be drier. We hope that, in the first place, the Manual will help you to recognize the conditions of light, heat and humidity in which the contents of a house can exist safely.

In the second place, the Manual tries to explain how to dust, handle, move and store the various categories of objects to be found in a historic house. More than common sense is needed, as will be clear to those who have ever benefited from the advice of skilled conservators.

Thirdly, the Manual contains a lot of important 'don'ts', the reasons for which we hope the reader will understand. We have tried to explain why 'do-it-yourself' treatment is no longer advisable for old and fragile objects. The phrase 'consult an expert' recurs constantly in these pages, and it cannot be stressed enough that repairs carried out by unsupervised amateurs will almost always cause more damage in the long run than the natural process of decay.

The conservator's job is increasingly separated from that of the traditional craftsman, partly because of the advance in scientific knowledge of what might be called the chemistry of decay and partly because of its long-term purpose. In his quest after the causes of decay the conservator is making scientific inquiry into a new field, just as is the specialist in geriatrics who asks what causes human decay in old age, and how he can arrest or alleviate it. The cabinet-maker, the clock-maker, the bookbinder and other craftsmen may all be concerned with new objects or with maintenance, while the conservator is concerned with preserving something old as much as possible in its original state. It may well make practical sense to replace an old member of a chair with a stronger one of different wood or to strengthen it with chocks and screws; but the first principle of the conservator is to save whatever can be saved and only to replace what must be replaced – and then always in materials identical to those originally used, keeping meticulous records of the work done.

It is up to the Trust to take every advantage of advances in the knowledge of conservation where they can be useful to us, and it is indeed with the generous help of many professional conservators that this Manual has been written. Some of these are full-time employees of the National Trust, most notably the Trust's Deputy Surveyor of Conservation, Hermione Sandwith, and the Trust's Housekeeper, Sheila Stainton, who first conceived the idea of this book and have played a major part in putting it together. Much valuable advice has also been given by the Historic Buildings Secretary, Martin Drury, and his predecessor, St John Gore, and the book has been edited for publication by the Architectural Adviser, Gervase Jackson-Stops. The earliest demonstration of good housekeeping came from Waddesdon Manor where Colonel Waller, the Administrator, and Miss Griffin, the Curator, were kind enough to arrange a demonstration of the de Rothschild methods and traditions in the spring of 1977. Other contributors include James Bellchambers, Jonathan Betts, Stephen Calloway, Pamela Clabburn,

Alec Cobbe, Briony Eastman, Andrew Garrett, Paul Giudici, Jean Glover, Mary Goodwin, Roy Hale, Keith Harding, John Hart, John Hartley, Martin Holden, Sheila Landi, Herbert Lank, Judy Larney, John Larson, Paul Levi, Helen Lloyd, Jane McAusland, Jane Mathews, Jim Murrell, Andrew Naylor, Victoria Pelham Burn, Viola Pemberton Pigott, Nicholas Pickwood, Trevor Proudfoot, James Robinson, Hugh Routh, Francesca Scoones, Phillip Stevens and Muriel Winship. Without help in the early stages from Norman Brommelle and Jonathan Ashley-Smith of the Victoria and Albert Museum, and Garry Thomson of the National Gallery, the Manual would never have got off the ground. Help has also been received from members of staff of the British Library, the British Museum, the Hamilton Kerr Institute, the National Maritime Museum, the Science Museum, the Tate Gallery, the Victoria and Albert Museum and the International Wool Secretariat.

The lists of equipment and suppliers given in the appendices at the end of the book are by no means exhaustive, nor can the National Trust take any responsibility for goods purchased from these firms or guarantee the availability of any items. The lists are given in good faith, based on the information available at the time of going to press, and we hope that it will be possible to widen and update them in future editions of the Manual.

It is very much regretted that the staff of the National Trust cannot give opinions on objects or advice on their conservation. The different departments of the British Museum and the Victoria and Albert Museum in London, and some of the larger provincial museums, can be consulted at certain stated hours during the week, and the names and addresses of bodies concerned with conservation work can be found in the *Conservation Sourcebook*, published by the Crafts Council (1979).

Finally, it remains to be said that the *National Trust Manual of Housekeeping* came into being specifically to answer some of the problems posed by the regular and ever-increasing opening of historic houses to the public. While many of its lessons are applicable to smaller private houses and collections, the mention of druggets and ropes, display cases and room stewards, must be excused by those who have the good fortune not to need them.

Like all textbooks, the Manual may occasionally seem dull and dry but, like all good textbooks, it will repay careful reading. We hope that you will refer to it often, and so help to improve the standard of conservation of the heritage that has been given to each and every one of us.

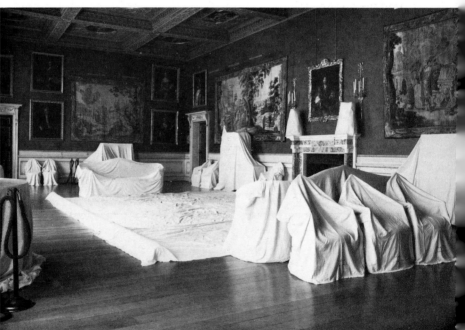

2 and 3. The Saloon at Chirk Castle as normally shown and as 'put to bed' for the winter

INTRODUCTION

BY JOHN CORNFORTH

Get the great dining-room in order as soon as possible. Unpaper the curtains, take the covers off the couch and the chairs, and put the china figures on the mantelpiece immediately. And set them o'nodding as soon as his lordship comes in, d'ye hear, Trusty.

To find such instructions to a servant in a mid-eighteenth-century comedy – the play is George Colman's *The Clandestine Marriage* of 1766 – suggests how widely practices of good housekeeping were understood at the time; the quotation is only unusual in the reference to paper being used to cover curtains. But certainly paper covers for chairs were known, even if none survive. Inevitably, the history of housekeeping with all its fascinating intricacies has been forgotten, because no one bothered to write it down while traditions were maintained by well-established staffs, presided over by a well-upholstered housekeeper. And now we are faced not only by the disappearance of the staff, but by an unprecedented demand to see houses and their contents. It is the combination of the two that has posed such problems for the National Trust.

Despite what one is led to believe, staff problems are not a twentieth-century phenomenon, for letters and diaries of earlier generations are full of grumbles about bad servants, servants who would not get up on cold mornings, servants who left, the difficulty of replacing them and their demands for exorbitant wages – which strike us as inhumanly small. In a country house the servants would have waited on the family and on each other, but their care of the house was just as important. In this they were in a kind of unstated partnership with the owner, who was quite likely not to use the front door or the principal rooms every day and would accept that, for normal living, second-best was good enough.

The best was what was wanted in the principal rooms, but it was very expensive, and so it was only used on special occasions and was expected to last for several generations, so as to become part of a family's dignity and evidence of its antiquity. Thus great care was taken to protect objects, particularly against light, and houses were often shut up for lengthy periods while a family was in London for political or social reasons. Indeed many of

4. *The Blue Curtain* by Adriaen van der Spelt, dated 1658. The curtain and rod painted in *trompe l'œil* show what was a common method of protection for pictures and water-colours in the seventeenth and eighteenth centuries

the houses that are now most noted for their tapestries and materials, like Hardwick in Derbyshire, or Boughton (not NT) in Northamptonshire, are those that were least used and so least subjected to light.

Sixteenth- and early-seventeenth-century pictures often had curtains in front of them and tapestries continued to do so as late as 1939 in some exceptionally well-cared-for houses. Fine beds with hangings of damask or needlework also had case curtains and these were often of the same colour as the show material or its lining but of a cheaper, more hard-wearing material. Chairs and settees also had case covers; indeed, as can be seen at Erddig, they often had both everyday covers and a top cover against dust and light as well. Carpets often had druggets to protect them against heavy wear as well as light, and some of these were like heavy damask tablecloths. Chandeliers had bags and mirror frames had covers, while pieces of gilt and veneered or inlaid furniture were sometimes supplied with covers made of leather, or of heavy cotton, carefully lined and cut to fit. Like the case covers of chairs, these would be charged for as part of the original order.

The covers would be taken off the furniture when the family was in residence, but those on the chairs and settees and often the druggets on the carpets would be cheerfully accepted. Also, when the sun came round, blinds would be drawn and shutters closed whether or not there were people about, for it was considered that the protection of the contents of a house should come before the fleeting convenience of a family and its guests.

Opening a house to the public for a long season, year after year, obviously produces the need for a different kind of balance. Visitors must be shown what they have come to see, but if the reason is explained, they will readily appreciate why there are case covers on most of the chairs in a set, why a bed has case curtains, and why blinds are drawn. It can be justified in practical terms – the responsibility of today for tomorrow – and in historical terms too. (Many visitors would surely be intrigued to be told that servants were instructed not to touch gilding.) It can be explained that, in order to show fragile objects in the context of a house, it is necessary to have a code of conduct that includes, for example, reducing the level of light, for otherwise the objects would deteriorate, or even disappear, and that the alternative is to remove them to the neutral but controlled conditions of a museum.

Perhaps we do not always realize what a privilege it is to see so many of our country houses complete with their original contents, a sight that can hardly be paralleled anywhere else in the world, and cannot be re-created. How vital it is, therefore, that the traditions of housekeeping should not just be maintained, or revived where they have slipped, but improved in the light of modern scientific knowledge. It is, without doubt, the only way in which future generations will be able to share our experience to the full.

He had been eight years upon a project for extracting sun-beams out of cucumbers, which were to be put into vials hermetically sealed, and let out to warm the air in raw inclement summers ...

Jonathan Swift, *Voyage to Laputa*, 1726

... The greatest event was that Mrs Jenkyns had purchased a new carpet for the drawing room. Oh the busy work Miss Matty and I had in chasing the sunbeams as they fell in an afternoon right down on this carpet through the blindless window! We spread newspapers over the places and sat down to our book or our work and lo! in a quarter of an hour the sun had moved and was blazing away on a fresh spot, and down again we went on our knees to alter the position of the newspapers.

Mrs Gaskell, *Cranford*, 1853

CHAPTER ONE

THE RIGHT ENVIRONMENT

5. Window curtains in tatters in the Tapestry Room at Erddig, showing the harmful effects of light

·❖ THE RIGHT ENVIRONMENT ❖·

LIGHT

The damage caused by light can never be reversed. Any light, whether strong or weak, will cause damage. A strong light will produce the same amount of damage in one hour as a light which is half as strong in two hours. It is essential, therefore, not only to reduce light levels but to cut down the time an object is exposed to light. This is the only preventive action that can be taken to prolong its life.

Where shutters and sun-blinds are in use, opening a house to the public seven days a week, rather than five, increases the deterioration of exhibits by exposure to light by 40 per cent.

In a house, the things that are most sensitive to light are textiles, water-colours and all works on paper (including wallpaper), miniatures, dyed leather (including leather wall hangings), fur, feathers, and most natural exhibits, such as stuffed birds. Oil paintings and ivory are sensitive to light. Only metals, stone, glass, ceramics, jewellery, enamel and wood are insensitive to light, and even wood will suffer a change of surface colour.

Visible light is only part of the spectrum of radiation filtering down through the earth's atmosphere. Beyond the visible spectrum at one end are the ultraviolet rays, which lie next to the blue end of the spectrum seen by the human eye, and at the other end, beyond the visible red, are infra-red rays.

Light is a source of energy and chemical change requires energy. Chemical change, which causes deterioration, is, therefore, brought about by exposing an object to light. Fading and other changes of colour occur. The energy of light is much greater at the ultraviolet end of the spectrum, but the warmer-coloured, yellow-red light at the infra-red end is a greater source of heat, and heat dries out an object. (For the effect of heat on the moisture content of an object see Heating, p. 24.)

Ultraviolet rays do a lot of harm, and as the eye is insensitive to them, since they lie outside the visible spectrum, they contribute nothing to the quantity of light entering a room. Ideally, the glass of all windows should be treated with UV-absorbent varnish or film (see Appendix 1, p. 240). We should then get rid of the damaging UV rays and be left with only two problems: visible daylight and artificial light. (For museum-recommended light levels, see Appendix 2, Light meters, p. 245.)

Daylight

All sunlight, whether direct or reflected, is damaging. Light falling on an object must, therefore, be reduced. *It is not only direct sunlight that causes damage.*

6. Sun-curtains in the Long Gallery, Hardwick

Methods of protection

Shutters, sun-blinds and sun-curtains can all be used to protect the contents of a house from the damaging effects of light, and ideally the glass of all windows except for stained glass should be treated with UV-absorbent varnish or film (see Appendix 1, pp. 239ff.).

Electric light

The intensity of artificial light is more easily controlled than daylight so that some things, which are particularly light-sensitive, may be shown more safely by electric light. However, care should be taken to avoid glare because the eye will adapt itself to the brighter light and not see the less brightly lit object adequately.

Ordinary electric light bulbs (tungsten incandescent lamps)

Tungsten lamps produce almost no ultraviolet radiation but heating can be a problem. The amount of light should be kept as low as possible and the source of light far enough away so that the surface of the exhibit does not heat up from the lamp and, most of all, is not subjected to uneven heat from a spot of light striking the surface. Exhibits can become overheated if these bulbs are fitted below a shelf.

Fluorescent tubes

Fluorescent tubes are available in a wide range of 'daylight' colour tones. They heat up less than tungsten lamps but ultraviolet radiation from un-shielded fluorescent tubes can cause damage.

Never install a fluorescent tube without fitting a UV-absorbent jacket (see Appendix 1, p. 241). The ballast unit of a fluorescent tube should be outside a showcase because of the heat it emits.

Spotlights

Occasionally spotlights are used in houses for special exhibits. With all spotlights there are problems of intensity of light and particularly heat. Specialist advice should be sought.

ATMOSPHERIC CONDITIONS

The atmospheric conditions of a room generate problems of humidity and temperature, which are closely related, and pollution. Pollution is created in industrial areas but winds spread the polluted air throughout the country.

The widespread nature of this hazard can be shown by the fact that the acid in the atmosphere in Norway is generated by factories in Britain. The salt air from the sea is another source of trouble. Masses of visitors in a room add to pollution and increase the relative humidity and risk of condensation.

Unfortunately, there is nothing practical that can be done about pollution, but sudden changes of temperature and extremes of heat and cold should be avoided. Because the human body, a table and a cucumber – most objects in fact – are made up of water, to a greater or lesser degree, they contract with loss of water and then expand again. They are subjected to a daily fatigue cycle of expanding and contracting with changing humidity.

Some objects, for example the human body or a piece of wood, can recover from quite severe loss of water. However, even wood does not return exactly to its original size and may crack under the strain of severe movement.

Providing ideal conditions would be fairly simple if artefacts were made up of only one material, but panel paintings, for example, are made up of wood (the support), gesso (the ground) and paint layers and varnish. All react differently to loss of water, and thus extremes of expansion and contraction cause the layers to lose their adhesion, and the painting to become unstable; in severe cases, the wooden support will crack as well.

Humidity

Nearly everything in a house is wholly or partly made from organic material. Even in good conditions these objects are constantly losing and gaining water, and this can be blamed on the air. When the air is dry it absorbs moisture from the objects, and when it is humid, they can make up lost moisture by absorbing it from the air. Except for the danger of mould growth, it is safer for humidity to be on the high side rather than too low.

It is important for the safety of an exhibit to know the amount of moisture in the air and this can be measured on a scale from 0 to 100. At 0, the air is bone dry, and at 100, the air is completely saturated with water and moisture begins to condense upon cold surfaces. Hot air holds more water than cold. When people talk about relative humidity (RH), they are not simply measuring the amount of water in the air, but measuring the degree to which the air is saturated.

A humidity of 50–60 per cent is ideal for most objects. Above 70 per cent there is a possibility of mould growth. Below 40 per cent paper and water-absorbent materials become brittle, and wood shrinks, causing it to warp and crack.

For hygrometers, for measuring relative humidity, see Appendix 2, p. 246.

7 and 8. Problems caused by extremes of humidity: (left) panelling split as a result of central heating; (below) mould growth on the surface of a water-colour

Temperature

In controlling RH levels, the temperature is important, but heat is surprisingly difficult to control. In summer, light is a factor in increasing temperature, and by excluding light through keeping shutters closed and sun-blinds down for as many hours of the day as possible, the temperature of a room may be kept more stable.

Heating

In this country central heating has become perhaps the largest single factor in causing damage to the contents and even to the structure of our houses. As human beings we can accommodate ourselves to considerably higher temperatures than artefacts because we drink more liquids if we become hot. Objects cannot adapt by taking in moisture unless it is present in sufficient quantities in the atmosphere; central heating prevents this because it heats and dries the air, which dehydrates them. Central heating can lower the RH from the ideal 50–60 per cent down to as low as 20 per cent.

In houses open to the public, central heating should be used to provide a little background heat to maintain a low and even temperature over twenty-four hours. This should not exceed 15°C (60°F). When the house is closed, if it is too expensive to keep the heating on permanently at low, then it is better to have no heating during the day, when temperatures rise naturally, and to have a low heat on throughout the night.

The most damaging use of central heating is when a house is very cold during the week and it is then heated suddenly at weekends, or when a room may be subjected to a dramatic change of temperature for a couple of days in the middle of winter for a hunt ball or a concert. To accommodate these events with the least damage to the contents of the house, bring the heat up gradually during the week before the event. For this reason, all central-heating systems must be fitted with thermostats that work. Remember that each visitor gives off as much heat as a 100 watt bulb, so a room can heat up considerably during a concert.

A house will be more efficient and cost less to maintain and less in bills for conservation work if the heating system for the showrooms of a house and the heating systems for its inhabitants are quite separate.

Avoid any sort of paraffin or Calor-gas heaters which produce a great deal of moisture – roughly equivalent in quantity to the fuel they burn. The excess moisture cools quickly with a risk of condensation. Paraffin and Calor-gas heaters also produce minute quantities of sulphur dioxide as a by-product. This is the common pollutant gas in the atmosphere and it reacts with moisture to produce minute quantities of sulphuric acid that attack objects.

Condensation

Condensation depends mainly on what happens when the temperature of a solid surface is lower than that of the air round it. In a heated room on a cold night, the external wall may be affected by condensation and anything hanging on this wall may suffer.

When the air cools in contact with a cold surface, it can no longer carry so much water, and water and dust are deposited.

When condensation occurs, on windowsills, for example, it should be wiped off so as to avoid water stains; artefacts should never be kept in places where there is a danger of condensation.

Pictures or other objects such as weapons and armour that may be hanging on an external wall should have corks fixed to the back of them, so that there is a passage of air between the back of the objects and the wall.

Ventilation

A sufficient circulation of fresh air is the best way of preventing mould growths. Still air is very like stagnant water in that it encourages the growth of bacteria, and conversely moving air or running water tends to discourage their growth.

It is, therefore, important to open windows in fine weather at regular intervals throughout the year. It is not necessary to open all the windows, but only a strategic few, chosen to encourage the circulation of fresh air. If doors are left open they should have door stops to prevent banging. Common sense will dictate that windows should not be open in high winds or in unsuitable weather conditions such as rain, snow, fog or mist.

Knowing I lov'd my books, he furnish'd me from mine own library with volumes that I prize above my dukedom.

Shakespeare, *The Tempest*, 1623

Books are not absolutely dead things, but do contain a potency of life in them to be as active as that soul was whose progeny they are . . .

Milton, *Areopagitica*, 1644

CHAPTER TWO

BOOKS AND DOCUMENTS

9. The library at Dunham Massey

·✤ BOOKS ✤·

It cannot be emphasized too strongly how necessary it is to be careful whenever handling books. A moment's carelessness can ruin a book whose interest and value may well lie in the fact that it has survived undamaged for centuries. A leather binding is not a guaranteed indication of value, and some of the most interesting books may look most unimpressive. A tattered paper wrapper may well be of greater value and almost certainly of greater interest than an ordinary gold-tooled leather binding. So equal care should be taken with every book, however unprepossessing it may appear. Never let the routine nature of much of the work which has to be done to books result in loss of concentration. The too-generous application of the leather dressing can stain leather permanently, and a moment's clumsiness with a duster can cause a lot of damage.

In houses open to the public, there are likely to be books whose condition or value makes it advisable to keep them out of the showrooms. If it is at all possible, shelving should be provided in some part of the house where these special books can be adequately housed. To make it easier to keep a check on the condition of all the library material in a house, and to make it available for use, the material must be protected, accessible and sorted. Sorting will normally involve the relocation of material, and can only be accomplished by the provision not only of extra shelving, but of carefully labelled boxes for some of the more ephemeral material which most houses contain. Such rehousing, in decent conditions, will make the material accessible both for use and periodic examination. It is a case where organization and conservation can be made to serve each other's interests, and where neither is entirely effective without the other. Sorting and classifying material should if possible be carried out under the supervision of a qualified librarian.

SHELF LIST

When cataloguing or carrying out conservation work on the library of a historic house, books should not be moved from the shelves until they have received their shelfmarks. The order in which they are arranged may be of historic interest.

A list of all books, arranged in shelf order, is compiled for every National Trust house for use during routine checks on lost or misplaced volumes. If a system has been used in the library, for historic reasons this should be retained; otherwise a new listing should be made. This is work which can be done by amateurs, and is not to be confused with the cataloguing undertaken by a professional librarian.

To make a shelf list, the bookcases in the library must be divided up into bays, or vertical banks of shelves. There may be two or more bays within a single bookcase, but the width of each bay is defined by the length of the individual shelves, and the bays will be divided one from the other by a vertical member. If a single bookcase contains three bays and there is no existing system of numbering, or lettering, then each bay can be numbered from left to right, 1, 2, 3.

The books are now ready to receive their shelfmarks, which should be made in pencil on the first plain paper leaf in the book, putting the marks, as far as possible, in the same place in each book. Always write lightly in a book as heavy pressure will mark the leaf below, and may damage some soft papers. Each volume in a multi-volume set should be given a different number.

Any existing shelfmarks must be left undisturbed and not rubbed out. If the new mark might be confused with the old, then draw brackets lightly, in pencil, round the old mark.

Starting from the top shelf of a bay, work through the books from left to right on the shelf, writing in each book three separate numbers:

bay number　　　　shelf number　　　book number.

The first book down from the top shelf would therefore be marked 1.a.1. The third book from the second shelf down of the second bay would be marked 2.b.3, and so on. As each book is given its shelfmark, the mark, followed by the title and author of the book (abbreviated if necessary) should be entered in the shelf list.

If a bookcase of three bays has already been given the letter A, the bays can be lettered from left to right A1, A2, A3. This would be followed in the usual way by the shelf number and the book number, A1.a.1 and A2.b.3.

Within each library there may well be a need to adapt any system to suit local peculiarities of library arrangement, but it is important that once each bay has been identified, a neatly drawn plan of the library, with each bay marked on it, be kept with the completed shelf list.

If it should ever prove necessary to move a book after it has received its shelfmark, do not rub out the shelfmark, as this will be the only record of where the book was formerly placed. Instead put brackets round it, and enter the shelfmark of the new location. Remember also to change the shelfmark in the shelf list.

CLEANING – ROUTINE CARE

It is best to take out all the books on a single shelf so that the woodwork can be inspected and dusted. It will make the job easier if there is a strong table near by to put the books on.

Never attempt to remove dust from the tops of books by banging the books together.

Hold the book firmly by the fore-edge to keep it closed, otherwise you will simply drive the dust into the book. Gently brush along the top edge of the book with a clean dry hogshair fitch – or use a shaving brush (see fig. 1). Dust trapped in front of the headband should be gently brushed out towards the fore-edge.

Fig. 1. Dusting a book

If it is noticed that dust has got on to the pages of a book, as is often the case when the paper has cockled slightly and opened up the top edge of a book, it may be brushed out very carefully, page by page, with a soft sable brush or ponyhair fitch.

Do not attempt to hurry this work; hands must be washed frequently to avoid transferring dirt from one book to another.

As always, particular care should be taken of damaged and fragile books, which should be set aside if they cannot be handled safely.

Dust on the sides of the book or the spine can easily be cleaned off with a duster, making sure that you are holding the loose corners of the duster in your hand so that they cannot catch on the book.

Where books have a thick layer of dust, it is best if they undergo an initial cleaning as they are removed from the shelves and before they are looked at, moved, or receive any other treatment. Use a Hoover Dustette equipped with the brush attachment. A piece of gauze, nylon net or a similar material should be placed across the tube behind the brush to prevent any small pieces of leather, headbands, etc., being sucked into the vacuum cleaner.

Follow the instructions given above for holding the book closed and for cleaning the headband.

When doing routine dusting look out for mould, woodworm, silverfish, mice and other pests.

Dog-ears

Dog-eared pages allow dust to penetrate a book, and they should be turned back. The crease left in the page will be evidence of their location. If they are brittle, however, they are better left alone, but comparatively little paper of pre-nineteenth-century date will be brittle. Dog-ears should be distinguished from a turned-in corner that preserves the original dimensions of the sheet of paper, having been turned in before the edges of the book were ploughed or guillotined. These should be left undisturbed, as they provide important evidence of the book's make-up and history.

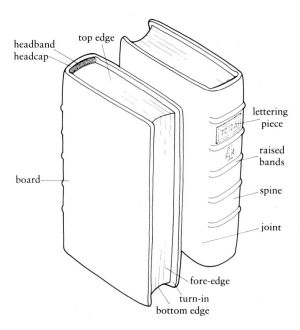

Fig. 2

Maps and documents

These are best left alone folded into a book. They should be examined with great care, and only when necessary, because the paper will frequently tear along the folds, especially where a fold is curved over the opening of a book.

Books with ties

Books which still retain their *silk or linen ties* on the fore-edges should be handled with great care. Do not attempt to tie and untie them as they are usually very fragile. Unless the book is boxed, it is safest to tuck the ties inside the boards before reshelving the book. (See fig. 2 for terminology.)

Loose material

There are two categories of loose material: those items that have become detached from the book, such as headbands, lettering pieces, etc., and those items which have been inserted into the book, in the way of bookmarks, notes, etc. It is important that items in both categories are preserved and not divorced from the books they come from.

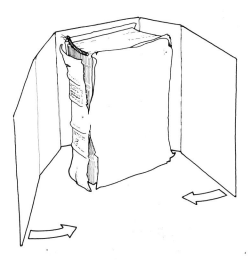

Fig. 3. A protective card wrapper

Loose boards and spines

Loose or detached boards and spines should be neatly bound with a soft tape to hold them together. This also serves as a warning that they are damaged. When tying the tapes use a bow, as other knots, being hard to untie, will tempt people to force them off over the end of the book, with the consequent likelihood of damaging the leather. *Never* use string or elastic bands to hold books together, for these will damage the books.

Card wrappers can be made to protect damaged books, as shown in fig. 3. Use acid-free lightweight board and tie the wrapper round the book with tape.

If, in cleaning and handling books, lettering pieces, headbands, etc., become detached, they should be placed in envelopes clearly marked with the shelfmark and short title of the book, and these envelopes should be kept together where they can easily be found when books are removed for repair. Attempts should not be made to stick them back unless someone working in the house has been shown how to do this work by a professional book conservator.

No bits of paper inserted into a volume, however apparently unimportant, should be thrown away. They should be kept, as they may have a bearing on the history of the book or the house.

Bookmarks, notes, etc., should be left in the books in the same places where they were found. As they may be of significance, record the page number where they are to be found, and the short titles and shelfmarks of the books. (A notebook might usefully be kept in each library for this purpose, and to record other points of interest noticed by those working on the books.) If for any reason such material is removed from books, place it in an envelope with the page number, short title and shelfmark clearly marked on it.

HANDLING

Books are easily damaged by careless handling, especially if they are already in a fragile state. Safe handling is mostly a matter of common sense, but the following guidelines may be helpful.

Removal from shelves

Never pull a book out by putting your fingers over the top of the spine; this may well pull the headband and headcap away from the spine (see fig. 4). Never pull a book out by gripping the back with your fingernails, as this may

Fig. 4   Fig. 5

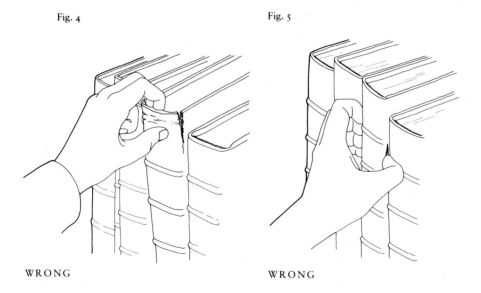

WRONG   WRONG

scratch it (see fig. 5). If there is room above the book, reach over the top of the book to the fore-edge and then pull it out (see fig. 6). If there is not room, push back the books on either side of the one to be removed, to expose enough of its spine to allow you to get a firm grip on it (see fig. 7).

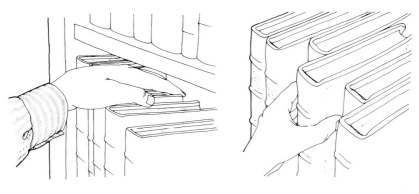

Fig. 6   Fig. 7

Books must never be so tightly packed in a shelf that it is difficult to move them. When removing a large heavy book from a shelf, grasp its bottom edge as it is pulled out of the shelf so as to be ready to take its weight (see fig. 8).

Fig. 8

Carrying books

Never carry more books than you can comfortably hold firmly in both hands (see fig. 9). A small book sliding around on top of a large one is always in danger of falling off. Even when moving large quantities of books, resist the temptation to take on more in weight or size than you can manage easily (see fig. 10). Should it ever be necessary to move books further than just across the room or into the next-door room, and certainly if stairs have to be negotiated, the books should be moved in tough boxes, with the books lying on their sides. Never force books into the box, and never pack in more than the person who is to carry the box can manage.

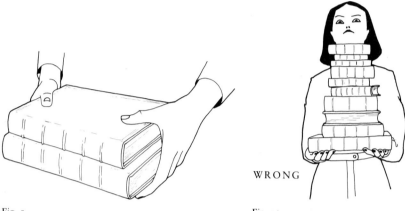

WRONG

Fig. 9   Fig. 10

Always treat books which are badly damaged, or bound in fragile materials such as silk or paper, with extreme care, and never pile them up on top of each other. Books covered in dust should not be opened until they have been cleaned, or the dust will get into the book and dirty the pages. (See Cleaning – routine care, p. 30.)

WRONG

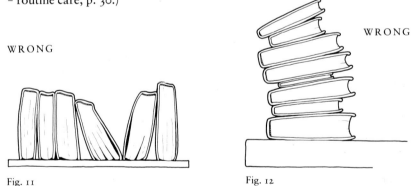

WRONG

Fig. 11   Fig. 12

Stacking books

Never support books on their fore-edges as this will damage the structure of a book and loosen the binding (see fig. 11). Keep books well away from liquids – vases of flowers, cups of coffee and so on. Books should not be stacked in tall piles, as these are easily knocked over (see fig. 12); keep books with metal clasps or bosses separate (see fig. 13).

WRONG

Fig. 13

Transporting books

The books, whether damaged or not, should be wrapped in clean paper and packed in tough cardboard boxes padded with blankets or polystyrene blocks so that the books cannot slide around in the box. The box should then be placed in the transporting vehicle in such a position that sudden stops, corners, etc., will not displace it. Putting books loose on the back seat of a car is an invitation to disaster.

If at all possible, books should not be sent by post, nor left in cars or vans overnight.

SHELVING AND STORAGE CONDITIONS

If the conditions in which books are kept are inadequate, the books will deteriorate on the shelves. A regular check should be kept on the light, temperature and humidity levels in the rooms in which books are kept.

Light

Light will degrade and discolour the organic materials from which books are made. The stronger the light and the longer the exposure to light, the greater the damage. Blinds should be fitted to the windows of libraries, and shutters closed whenever the room is not in use. Ultraviolet-absorbent varnish or film should be applied to the window glass. Fluorescent light fittings in storage rooms should be fitted with UV-absorbent sleeves.

Temperature

As a general rule, the temperature of a room in which books or documents are kept should be as low as practicable, though not so low as to allow condensation to form. The temperature should not be allowed to rise above 15°C (60°F). It is important to avoid fluctuations of temperature, as such fluctuations can be more damaging than a constant temperature which is slightly higher than desirable. It is important that the temperature in the relevant rooms is measured and recorded at regular intervals in order to find out what improvements may need to be made. A maximum/minimum thermometer read at the same time each day would give some idea of fluctuations of temperature within each twenty-four-hour period.

Relative humidity

Books, being made almost entirely of organic materials, need a certain amount of moisture. Excessive dryness will lead to the gradual embrittlement of paper, leather and vellum, but excessive moisture will lead to the loosening of starch- and gelatine-based adhesives, and, if there is inadequate ventilation, to mould growth (see Ventilation, below).

The relative humidity of the air around the books should not fall below 55 per cent nor rise above 65 per cent, and regular readings should be made and recorded. Readings should be taken at different points in the room, as conditions may well vary between one part and another, especially in large rooms.

Ventilation

It is important to ensure that not only the rooms where books are kept but also the shelves in which they are kept are properly ventilated.

Inadequate ventilation, coupled with excessive moisture, will result in mould growth. Mould spores will always be present in the air in the houses, but they will only germinate if the right conditions exist.

In some cases a fair amount of ingenuity, and possibly expense, will be needed to open up air passages without disturbing the appearance of the shelving. However, the importance of ventilation, especially where there are presses against outside walls, cannot be over-emphasized. Unchecked mould growth can cause hundreds of pounds worth of damage to a single book, and will eventually destroy the book altogether.

Ventilation is needed in two places – behind the books and behind the bookcases, especially when the bookcase is against an outside wall. Ventilation behind the books can usually be provided quite easily by leaving the shelves 2.5 cm (1 in) narrower than the side members by shaving off approximately 2.5 cm from the back of each shelf. If the shelves are fixed irremovably, then 2.5 cm diameter holes can be drilled along the back of the shelves at

10 cm (4 in) intervals. Ventilation behind the bookcases should take the form of an air space at least 2.5 cm wide between the backing boards of the case and the wall. To be effective, there must be gaps at top and bottom of the case as well, to allow air to move behind the case. The bottom shelf of the case, which is usually immovable, should be ventilated by drilling holes, as described above, and this should have the added effect of opening up ventilation behind the case (see fig. 14).

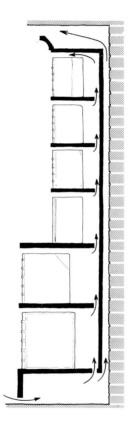

Fig. 14 Cross-section of a bookcase, showing passages for the movement of air

Drawers, cupboards and bookcases with glass doors are potentially dangerous unless adequately ventilated. In the case of documents and books in drawers and cupboards, removal to better storage elsewhere in the house may be the best answer.

Shelving

Most books are kept on shelves, and the shelving should be designed to provide secure, clean and convenient support for the books in it. Old shelving will frequently need modification to bring it up to standard and new shelving should be designed with the needs of the books in mind.

Unless books can be removed from and replaced on the shelves easily and without obstruction, there is always the likelihood of the books being damaged. The dead spaces formed at the end of some shelves by projecting fascia boards which overlap the front of the shelves should be filled up with wooden blocks. Any projections which are likely to come into contact with books should be removed or otherwise made harmless.

Many old bookcases have grooves cut in the sides to take the shelves at different levels, and these can often mark the books placed against them. This can be avoided by inserting a piece of acid-free mounting board between the book and the side member of the case.

Any surface that books come into contact with should be kept smooth, if not polished. A rough shelf or side member will wear down a binding very quickly.

Shelves which have sagged and have come into contact with books on the shelf below should be straightened and supported, perhaps by the insertion of a vertical member through the middle of the whole case.

Books must never be crammed tightly into shelves. This will scuff the leather, crush embossed bindings and lead to damage when attempts are made to move the books into or out of the shelves. Equally, books should not be so loosely packed that they will lean over at an angle. This will distort and strain the structures and eventually cause their breakdown. When correctly packed, the books should be easy to move in or out of the shelves, and yet give support to each other on the shelf. If there are not enough books to fill up a shelf, then wooden blocks should be used to take up the vacant space. If it is felt to be necessary, these can be given false leather spines, or painted in imitation of leather.

Books of different sizes

Large books should be kept next to large books and small books next to small. A large book with small books on either side will receive no support above the level of the small books, which will put a strain on its structure. But rearrangement of books on the shelves should only take place after the shelf list has been completed, recording the original position of the book.

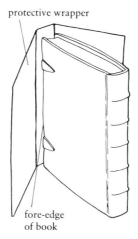

protective wrapper

fore-edge
of book

Fig. 15. A protective wrapper which leaves the spine visible – for books with clasps, ties and delicate tooling

Large books

Many large books should not be stood upright, as they are either too thick or too heavy to support their own weight. Where it can be seen that the fore-edge has begun to sag on to the shelf, the book should be laid flat. Do not, however, stack large numbers of books in a pile, as this may damage the books at the bottom. Alternatives include removing the books at risk to extra shelving, or inserting extra shelves in the library bookcase to take several volumes on their sides.

Books with clasps and bosses

Books with metal furniture, such as clasps, bosses, cornerpieces, etc., make very bad neighbours and will scratch and rip the leather on books on either side of them. As a temporary expedient, a piece of acid-free card should be placed against one board, folded round the fore-edge and on to the other board. This will leave the spine visible while covering the metalwork (see fig. 15).

New shelving

Most houses need some new shelving to house books displaced in putting the library shelving in order and to house books stored in inadequate conditions in attics, basements, etc. All such books should be placed on shelves in a dry, clean room where they are seen regularly and are available for use and examination. Books kept in boxes and piles on floors are inaccessible for both purposes. All the shelves apart from the bottom one should be adjustable. This allows for the most flexible and therefore most economical use of the space available. The exact means by which the adjustment is effected can be left to the carpenter, but a simple system of wooden pegs, with holes drilled at 2.5 cm (1 in) centres in the vertical members, is quite adequate. Care should be taken to ensure that, whatever system is used, no part of it will be likely to mark or damage the books. The shelves should be at least 2 cm (¾ in) thick, planed smooth, and not more than 76 cm (30 in) long. They should be at least 23 cm (9 in) deep for the most part, though shelving up to 46 cm (18 in) deep will have to be provided for larger books according to the demands of each collection.

If the new shelving is against an outside wall, it should be equipped with a back which must be held at least 2.5 cm (1 in) away from the wall. Whether it is against an inside or an outside wall, there should be provision for an air passage behind the books within the bookcase. This is simply achieved by leaving the shelves 2.5 cm narrower than the side members. A hardwood should be used in preference to a softwood. Metal shelving should not be used, because of the danger of corrosion, nor should glass-fronted shelving.

Mould

Whenever mould is detected in books, a professional conservator should be informed immediately, so that appropriate action may be taken. However, there is no point in treating books with fungicide unless the conditions which gave rise to the mould are put right (see Ventilation, p. 38).

Insects

Excessive moisture may also provide the right conditions for such pests as silverfish, which will damage both leather and paper.

The creatures which cause the most damage to books are silverfish, booklice, leather beetles and the larvae of the common furniture beetle (woodworm). The first two live on the moulds which thrive in damp conditions, and are best controlled by ensuring that damp conditions do not occur. If they are found in any books, or shelving, then the source of the moisture giving rise to the mould on which they feed must be located and put right. Silverfish, especially, can cause extensive damage. The other two insects do not need damp conditions to thrive, though woodworm attack is encouraged by damp-softened papers, and a careful check must be made regularly for signs of infestation.

Treat infected shelves with Cuprinol low-odour insecticide fluid, but do not replace the books on treated shelves for at least three weeks.

Rats and mice will attack books if they are given the chance. The gelatine glue used on the spines of many books is particularly attractive to them (and dogs), but they will also eat vellum and leather and chew up paper for nesting material. A single mouse can ruin a fine book in a few hours, and the least sign of infestation must receive prompt and efficient attention.

SECURITY

Nylon lines stretched across the front of shelves can act as a deterrent, but care must be taken to ensure that the line does not come into contact with the books. Books should not be tied together in blocks as this is likely to damage the books at each end. A simple system of stringing lines between pieces of wood or hardboard placed between the ends of the shelves and the books at each end is quite effective and does not hamper unnecessarily the normal handling of the books (see fig. 16). Security systems which are inconvenient to use will be abused.

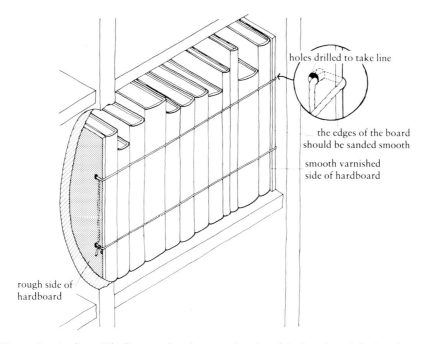

Fig. 16. Security lines. (The line must be taken over the edge of the boards, and the boards should stand slightly proud of the books on the shelf, so that the line does not come into contact with the books. The smooth sides of the boards should be coated with polyurethane varnish to prevent acid migration from the board to the neighbouring book.)

A shelf full of books, so that a gap would be obvious if one were taken, is also a deterrent. However, books should never be put under pressure in the shelves as this will damage them.

Where valuable books are kept, a steward should always be in the room if it is open to the public, and books on popular subjects, such as gardening, should be kept well out of reach.

Books of exceptional value should, whenever possible, be kept behind locked grilles, or, if this is not possible, removed for safe keeping to another part of the house, but only if the conditions there are satisfactory. Safes and strongrooms, especially those situated in basements, may well be damp and are frequently unventilated.

DISPLAY

The careless and poorly controlled display of books is a major source of damage and deterioration. Books and documents should only be displayed in rooms with proper controls over light levels, temperature and humidity. Display cases should be large enough to take the books comfortably, and must be properly ventilated. Ultraviolet-absorbent filters should be fitted to the glass and the cases should be solidly made so that accidental knocks from visitors do not shake the contents.

10. A cardboard stand made for a book on display

Whenever books are selected for display, whether in houses open to the public or on loan to other institutions, however prestigious they may be, the best course is to consult a professional book conservator, who will be able to give information on the safest way to exhibit the book. If the minimum conditions laid down are not provided, then the book should *not* go on display. Material such as light-sensitive, hand-painted initials and miniatures, and fragile bindings must only be displayed in very carefully controlled conditions, physical and atmospheric. Wherever possible, the use of photographs and facsimiles instead is to be recommended.

In many libraries books are left open in cases at one page throughout the season when the house is open. In many cases this will put a severe strain on the binding, as well as leading to the discoloration of the paper. Wherever possible good-quality reproductions should be used to avoid the risk of destroying a binding and spoiling its contents.

BOOKS IN NEED OF REPAIR AND SPECIAL CLEANING

No books should be repaired without the advice of a trained book conservator. There is also little point in embarking on expensive repair work on individual books before the storage conditions to which they will be returned are checked, and, if necessary, put right (see Shelving and storage conditions, p. 37).

A certain amount of cleaning, oiling and repair work can be done by amateurs but only under the supervision of a trained book conservator. Serious and permanent damage can be done by using inappropriate methods and materials.

·✤ DOCUMENTS ✤·

GENERAL REMARKS

Light and damp are the greatest causes of damage to documents. Most other damage is caused by careless handling or inadequate protection in storage and transport. The normal practice in the National Trust is for documents to be kept at the appropriate County Record Office, where they can be studied under supervision more easily than in the house.

Handling

All documents should be handled with the greatest care. Never pick up fragile documents with a finger and thumb but support them on a suitable backing sheet. When damage to a document is extensive, it should not be handled or unfolded or unrolled for inspection. The damage should be noted and the advice of a professional paper conservator sought.

If the document has a seal hanging loose, the seal on the document should be supported on thin card if it has to be moved or lifted on to another flat surface. If the seal is to be stored, use acid-free card (see Seals, p. 47).

No attempt should be made to change the sequence of the documents or remove fastening materials, as this may result in the loss of evidence of the original make-up of the documents.

Loose fragments from documents and maps should be placed in an acid-free envelope and kept with the documents concerned.

Large documents, maps and charts should be unrolled for inspection only if they are strong enough to stand this treatment and then only if a large smooth flat surface is available on which they can be supported. When unrolled, weights will be needed to keep the document flat.

Arrangements should be made to treat large documents, maps and charts so that they can be kept flat, as there is then less chance of damage occurring than when they have to be unrolled for inspection. Vellum documents are particularly unmanageable, especially when they are tightly rolled, as they frequently are.

Light

Strong light, particularly sunlight, causes rapid and irreversible deterioration to paper and also causes inks and pigments to fade. Sunlight should be excluded where documents are displayed and fluorescent tubes should *always* be fitted with UV-absorbent sleeves.

Ideally, documents should be kept in the dark, stored flat in special acid-free folders or solander cases.

Atmospheric conditions

Excessive heat shortens the life of paper. Documents should therefore never be stored near radiators or other sources of heat. In winter, the thermostat in a room where documents are kept should be set as low as possible without the room becoming too damp. Attics are only suitable for storage when well insulated.

Extremes in humidity and dryness should be avoided and a good circulation of air is essential for all documents.

Mould and mildew

Mould prevention requires that both temperature and humidity be kept within reasonable limits and a good circulation of air maintained.

If mould be discovered in paper documents, immediate action should be taken to improve the environmental conditions so that the mould cannot continue to propagate. The documents should be treated by a professional paper conservator.

Display

Facsimiles of documents can often be exhibited in place of valuable and irreplaceable originals

When originals are to be shown, display cases should be checked by a professional conservator at the design stage, as slight alterations could make all the difference to the safety of the document. The lighting and ventilation of display cases is particularly important. Documents on display should not be in contact with unsuitable materials.

ROUTINE EXAMINATION

Stored documents

Documents should be checked by a paper conservator and, if necessary, de-acidified before being stored.

Stored documents should be examined at regular intervals, say once a year.

A careful watch should be kept for paper and board that is becoming brown or brittle and for ink that is attacking the paper. (See Ink drawings, p. 165.)

Care should be taken to avoid documents being kept in close contact with unsuitable materials. Paper clips, staples and pins made from ferrous metals can rust and cause disfigurement and damage and should be removed, taking care to preserve at all times the original arrangements of the papers. Paper, vellum and parchment are attractive to rodents and a special watch should be kept for signs of mice.

Seals

Special care is necessary if the document has applied or pendant seals. Pendant seals should be protected by packing with loosely crumpled acid-free tissue paper (see Handling, p. 45). If in doubt, consult a conservator.

Cleaning

Never attempt to remove ingrained dirt from documents and maps. Cleaning should be left to a paper conservator. *Never* attempt to brush away dirt from written, decorated or illuminated areas.

*

See also Parchment and vellum, p. 173.

Then said another – 'Surely not in vain
My Substance from the common Earth was ta'en
That He who subtly wrought me into Shape
Should stamp me back to common Earth again.'

Fitzgerald, *Rubáiyát of Omar Khayyám*, 1859

CHAPTER THREE

CERAMICS

11. The State Closet at Beningbrough, showing porcelain displayed on a tiered overmantel of about 1715

·✤ CERAMICS ✤·

Ceramics is a broad term covering porcelain and all types of pottery.

ACCIDENTS AND REPAIRS

Ceramics will not deteriorate while awaiting repair so do not attempt to stick things together in the house but consult an expert conservator.

If an object is dropped never try and fit the pieces together to see if they join but wrap separately in tissue paper and put away safely, as more damage is done to the broken edges through being inexpertly handled and grated together.

Whenever possible, plates and other ceramics which have been riveted in the past should be properly repaired. Rivets can not only stain but also exert uneven pressure on the piece, particularly if some have worked loose.

HANDLING

Ceramics should be handled as little as possible.

Always look carefully at the object before attempting to lift it to see if there are any repairs that could part or bits that could be knocked off.

Always use both hands when picking up an object and make sure you have plenty of elbow room and are not liable to knock another object. *Never* reach over one object to pick up another.

Hairline cracks are difficult to detect by eye, so as well as taking care when picking objects up, be equally careful when putting them down again. This applies particularly where very hard surfaces, such as marble, are concerned, and as it really is necessary to concentrate when handling objects, do not turn round to talk to someone, particularly when putting something down. The distance above the table surface can easily be misjudged and too heavy an impact will cause breakage.

If objects are to be left out on a table for any length of time, make sure that they are placed well away from the edges so that they do not get accidentally knocked over by people passing by.

Always put an object down safely before answering the telephone or opening a door; it is advisable to have two people available for carrying whenever doors need to be opened, as this saves putting the object down and picking it up again.

Handles and rims

Never pick any object up by the handle. Use both hands when lifting a jug or cup. *Never* pick up a plate or bowl by the rim. Cradle it in both hands.

Lids

Test carefully any object with a lid to see if it is fixed or loose and do not pick it up by the knob or handle. If the lid is loose, remove it and place it somewhere safe before picking up the rest of the object. Even if it appears to be stuck or attached in some way, always support the lid with one hand when turning the object upside down.

Figurines: bocage

Objects with bocage or pieces sticking out should be picked up by supporting the base with both hands. Flowers, leaves, etc., particularly on Chelsea or Derby-type figurines, are extremely delicate and pieces can snap off quite easily if gripped.

Carrying objects

A basket, wicker if possible, is best for carrying objects, but baskets are expensive, bulky and difficult to store, so plastic-coated wire trays sold for storing vegetables or as freezer baskets can be used instead. Line them with felt and use plenty of tissue paper for padding.

Whether using a basket or tray, when carrying several articles at once make sure that the weight is evenly distributed so that it can be carried level and that there is enough packing between each item to prevent them rolling against each other should the basket be tipped or jolted.

Never try and squeeze in that one extra object to save a trip.

When dealing with an object of awkward size, or one which is very heavy or extensively repaired, be sure to have enough padding and, if necessary, have another person to assist. Do not have odd pieces hanging over the edges of the tray or basket.

STORING

Do not overcrowd shelves or cupboards and, wherever possible, place smaller objects in front of larger ones.

Make sure an object is dry before it is put away in a cupboard.

Before closing cupboard doors check that there is plenty of clearance and that the object will not get damaged.

Cups and bowls

Never stack cups and bowls one inside another. It is worth the expense to fit extra shelves, narrow and shallow, between existing ones, for accommodating smaller objects. It will save time as well as being safer for them.

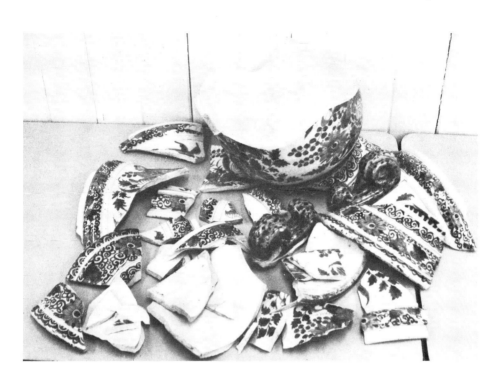

12 and 13. A Delft vase from Dyrham before, and after, repair

Plates

Never stack too many plates in a pile. Make sure that the plates in a pile are of the same shape and size. Never put a larger plate on top of a smaller one. Interleave a pile of plates with folded pieces of tissue paper to protect the surface of each plate. Deep soup plates often need thicker padding than tissue paper to give the necessary support.

Make sure that any metal hangers on plates are removed before storing.

ROUTINE CARE

Ceramics should be handled as little as possible. Every time an object is dusted it is at risk, so during the winter, when houses normally opened to the public are closed and where space is available, move all ornaments except clocks on to one table and cover them individually with paper hats made of acid-free tissue paper and pins, and marked with the inventory number. This avoids the need to dust and so considerably reduces the possibility of an accident. Another advantage is that the chimney pieces, shelves and occasional tables, etc., are clear, ready for the room to be spring-cleaned. Also, covering the objects for five months of the year when the house is closed may postpone the need for special cleaning for several years.

Hanging plates

Metal hangers (spring and clip type) are quite safe to use for hanging plates as long as the plate has no hairline or travelling cracks. The most important thing is to ensure that the hanger is the correct size for the plate. If it is too small, then obviously the plate will be put under stress.

Protect ceramic glaze from the metal clips by using strips of chamois leather or plastic tubing.

Mats

Some ceramics have rough bases which can scratch polished surfaces. Mats made out of chamois leather or suitably coloured felt can give protection. (See Ornaments, flowers and jardinières, p. 85.)

All flower vases should be stood on mats, even if placed on marble or stone-topped surfaces. Water can so easily spill and not be noticed, leaving marks on all types of surfaces.

SPRING-CLEANING

As with furniture, if the object looks clean and fresh no special cleaning is necessary. A careful dust with a soft duster or a hogshair brush should be enough. Occasionally, if builders have been working in the house or objects have come from a store, ceramics have to be washed.

Preliminary examination

Always examine the object very carefully before washing, as many old repairs were done with water-soluble adhesives which part relatively easily in warm water. Also consult a ceramics conservator before cleaning very dirty pieces, as over-painted areas may not be so obvious when the rest of the object is dirty, but could show up and be visually disturbing against a cleaner surrounding, making further restoration desirable.

Ceramics can be roughly divided into the following four categories:

Low-fired pottery or earthenwares (soft, porous)
For example, Neolithic, Greek, Roman and Chinese potteries; (tin-glazed) Islamic and Hispano-Moresque potteries, Italian majolica, French faience, Dutch delft and English delftwares; (lead-glazed) Islamic potteries, slipwares, Staffordshire potteries.

High-fired pottery or stonewares (non-porous)
Chinese Yueh ware and celadons; (salt-glazed) Rhenish and English stonewares; (lead-glazed) Staffordshire stonewares and creamwares; (unglazed) Wedgwood basalt and jasper wares.

Soft-paste 'imitation' porcelain (porous)
Medici, Capodimonte, Rouen, St Cloud, Mennecy, Vincennes, Bow, Chelsea, Derby, Worcester; bone china; (unglazed) Parian wares.

Hard-paste 'true' porcelain (non-porous)
Chinese and Japanese porcelains, Meissen, Vienna, Sèvres, Plymouth, Bristol; (unglazed) biscuit wares.

Low-fired potteries and soft-paste porcelains are fragile and porous; high-fired stonewares and hard-paste porcelains are generally more durable and non-porous.

Ceramics which should be cleaned with special care and attention

Porous and soft-paste ceramics

Porous and soft-paste ceramics should not be immersed, as dirty water absorbed through the base can cause staining. They also take a considerable time to dry out thoroughly, but they can be stood on a flat surface and cleaned using swabs of cotton wool.

Parian and biscuit ware

Parian and biscuit ware, which is usually white, is unglazed. The dirt is often more ingrained due to the unglazed surface, which makes it harder to clean. If the dirt does not respond to water and Synperonic N, consult an expert.

Gold decoration

Never immerse an object which has gold decoration. Gold sometimes comes away even when dusted so, with any form of cleaning, stop if the gold appears to be unstable.

Metal and ormolu mounts

Metal, especially ormolu, must not get wet. Ceramics which have ormolu mounts should be dusted and, if very dirty, the ceramics only cleaned with a slightly damp swab of cotton wool and dried immediately.

Washing

As it is often very difficult to see old repairs it is safest not to immerse the object but to stand it on the table and wash it with cotton-wool swabs, damp rather than wet, either held in the hand or made up by twisting cotton wool round a wooden cuticle-stick (which can be bought at any chemist). A soft bristle brush will usually deal with the more intricate parts that are difficult to get at.

Always keep one hand on the object when washing, as a support. Work from the top down, rinsing off as you go with a cotton-wool swab squeezed out in clean water. The water must be kept clean, which means changing it frequently.

While ideally ceramics should be washed near running water, it is often better to set up a trestle table in the room rather than carry the objects a great distance. Cover the table top with a piece of thin foam plastic 0.5–1 cm ($\frac{1}{4}$–$\frac{1}{2}$ in) thick, to soften the surface. Have plastic bowls and plenty of buckets for carrying water. Use both round and square bowls, as objects which can be turned around in a round bowl will not necessarily do so in a square one. Figurines, for example, are better washed in a round bowl, as allowance must be made for outstretched arms, branches and foliage, etc., which could easily be knocked. Protect the floor with dust-sheets. Do not use polythene sheeting on the floor as it is very slippery.

Always start with lukewarm water and only if this does not remove the dirt progress to lukewarm water with a very little Synperonic N. Afterwards rinse with clean water. (See Appendix 3, p. 250.)

Never use ordinary household detergents which contain harmful additives such as bleach. Fairy Liquid is a mild commercial detergent. *Never* use soap, as it will leave the object smeary.

Draining and drying

Lay objects down on foam-rubber sheets or squares, which should not be more than about 1 cm ($\frac{1}{2}$ in) thick. Be careful when putting objects down on the foam – if it is too thick, the object could topple over. Dry very gently with a soft linen tea towel or paper towels, taking care not to put excess pressure on any one area. To dry figures with a lot of bocage use a hair-dryer set at cold.

Accidents while washing

Should any object come apart, or an accident occur, finish the cleaning process of all the pieces, dry them thoroughly and wrap each of the pieces separately in tissue paper or soft paper towel. *Never* attempt to stick the bits together again.

Very dirty objects

If the object is exceptionally dirty it may be better to take it to a sink so that the dirty water can drain away. The less the object is handled the better. Make absolutely sure that the object is well clear of the taps, which can easily get in the way of taller objects. Wrap the taps round with old rags or dusters as a safeguard against an accidental knock. Line the bottom of metal, enamel or porcelain sinks with foam rubber. Make sure that the water is lukewarm.

Greasy dirt on glazed surfaces

A mixture of 50/50 white spirit and water, with one teaspoon of Fairy Liquid added to one pint of this mixture, makes a good cleaner for greasy dirt on glazed surfaces. Shake well before use and apply with a swab of cotton wool. Rinse well in clean water, using a damp cotton-wool swab. Use this treatment on rare occasions and only on glazed surfaces. Always try lukewarm water with a very little Synperonic N first, and if in doubt ask an expert conservator.

Stains

Never use household detergents or bleaches on ceramics to try to remove stains.

'Pray my dear', quoth my mother, 'have you not forgot to wind up the clock?' – 'Good G—!' cried my father, making an exclamation, but taking care to moderate his voice at the same time, – 'Did ever woman, since the creation of the world, interrupt a man with such a silly question?'

Laurence Sterne, *Tristram Shandy*, 1759-67

CHAPTER FOUR

CLOCKS AND WATCHES

14. At Anglesey Abbey, a fine automaton clock in pagoda style, ormolu case by Henry Borrell, London, *c.* 1810. The clock strikes the quarters, and at the hour one of four tunes plays as the plants slowly revolve and 'grow'

Clocks and watches should be kept out of extremes of temperature, humidity and airborne dust, which means away from direct sunlight, radiators, central-heating vents and positions near open fires. Windowsills, which are exposed to extreme changes of temperatures and where condensation might form, should also be avoided.

The ideal conditions for the wooden cases of clocks conflict with the needs of the metal mechanism, but a good compromise would be 45–65 per cent relative humidity, in a temperature not exceeding 15°C (60°F). The atmosphere should, of course, be as clean as possible.

As well as avoiding sudden changes in temperature and humidity, try to choose a position where the clock is least likely to have to be moved, and where it will be on a solid, stable base.

CARE AND MAINTENANCE

Unless an expert indicates otherwise, clocks and watches should be kept in good working order, although it is not recommended that any watch not in use be wound and run.

If a clock does not work, or begins to behave erratically, it should be *left stopped* until it can be inspected by a properly qualified clock-maker. There are very few capable of properly restoring and recording a rare clock; never trust the 'little man round the corner'.

Day-to-day care

Never try to repair, clean or oil clock or watch mechanisms or to clean the dials or brass case mounts in any way.

Dust the case with a clean, soft duster and avoid using proprietary glass cleaners which may contain ammonia.

If the case is of wood and needs polishing, use the National Trust's furniture polish (see Polishing, p. 86), making sure the case is steady and that there are no loose or projecting veneers or mouldings that could be 'snatched' by the cloth. Should parts become detached, put them in an envelope, marked with the inventory number, in the furniture 'bit box' so that they can be re-attached on the next visit of a furniture conservator.

Pieces removed from clocks and returned by the clock conservator should also be labelled and preserved for possible future reference.

Watch cases should be dusted but not polished as this would wear the surface. An occasional 'dusting' with a silver cloth is acceptable.

All clock cases should be kept locked and case keys, as well as those for winding, should be kept labelled and in one safe place. A board on a wall would be ideal.

Tower and stable clocks should be maintained only by a recommended company, on a contract basis.

Winding and setting

Each clock should have its own winding key, which should fit the squares in the clock snugly to avoid damage.

When winding keep the clock case steady with one hand and wind with care, especially towards the end. It is useful to remember the number of turns needed for each clock. Also, it is a good idea, if there are several eight-day clocks in the house, to choose one set day of the week on which to wind them all.

When setting the hands always move them clockwise, *never* anti-clock-wise.

On striking clocks, wait for the clock to finish striking before moving on; for example, if the clock is quarter striking, you should wait at each quarter hour until it has completed striking.

If for any reason the hands should jam, do not force them. This applies to all movable parts.

When winding a tower or stable clock always use the 'maintaining power' device, if present, to avoid damage to the escapement (fig. 17).

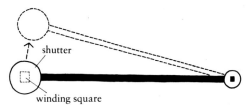

shutter

winding square

Fig. 17. 'Maintaining power' device

If hand setting on a tower or stable clock can only be achieved by disengaging the pallets of the escapement and letting the clock run freely, always keep the speed low, and *never* re-engage the pallets until the escape wheel is stationary.

Regulating

With pendulum controlled clocks, the pendulum bob must be lowered if running too fast and raised if running too slow.

Find the rating nut, usually below the bob, which, if turned clockwise

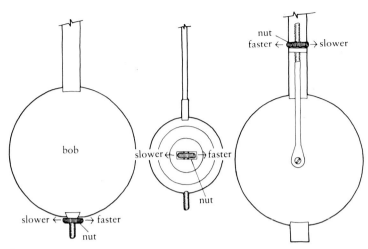

Fig. 18

(when looking down on the nut from above), lowers the bob to make the clock go slower and vice versa (fig. 18). Only a very small adjustment is usually necessary.

Some French pendulum clocks have a small square above the twelve on the dial, for fine regulating. This is useful as it saves having to move these often very cumbersome clocks. Use a small watch key, turning the square anti-clockwise to slow the clock down, and vice versa.

Clocks with platform escapements instead of a pendulum normally have a small lever to regulate the rate of the balance wheel, but this adjustment is better left to a qualified clock-maker.

HANDLING, TAKING DOWN AND SETTING UP

Avoid the handling, taking down and setting up of clocks. Consult an expert first; if handling is unavoidable, the advice given below must be followed.

Spring-driven clocks

Never pick up a clock by its carrying handle alone. Support it underneath as well in case the handle fails.

Platform escapement clocks, with balance wheels, may be moved carefully without fear of damage to the mechanism.

There is sometimes a pendulum-securing device on English pendulum spring clocks. It might take the form of a brass threaded knob, normally stored screwed into one of the case brackets, which should be unscrewed

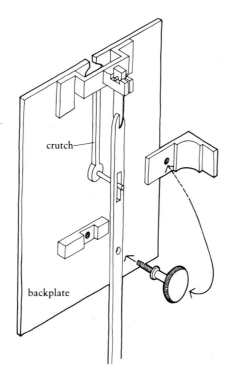

crutch

backplate

Fig. 19

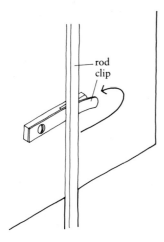

rod
clip

Fig. 20

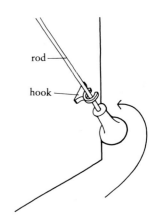

rod

hook

Fig. 21

and screwed over the pendulum rod into a central brass block (fig. 19) or there may be a similar device with a clip instead of a brass knob (see fig. 20). Sometimes, on earlier spring clocks with verge escapement, there is a C-shaped hook on one side of the plate, into which the pendulum rod can be placed (fig. 21).

Even without such devices, pendulum spring clocks with a crutch can be moved short distances if the dial of the clock is leant towards the carrier so that the pendulum is resting on the backplate of the movement.

If it is necessary to remove the pendulum, the movement can be stopped from 'tripping' (running faster than usual) by gently pushing a small wedge of paper behind the crutch (fig. 19). Beware of damaging the very delicate suspension spring of the pendulum, usually attached to the top of the pendulum rod in English clocks, but often attached to the movement in French clocks. It is not possible to remove the pendulum on verge clocks (see fig. 21).

Sometimes, especially in French clocks, it is necessary to remove the bell, if on the backplate, before the pendulum can be removed.

Setting up again involves procedures very similar to those for weight-driven clocks.

Weight-driven clocks (longcase, lantern clocks, etc.)

Proceed as follows if a weight-driven clock has to be moved, or if it is to be taken away for repair. Cotton gloves should be worn when stabilizing the movement so as to avoid leaving fingerprints on the metalwork (see Handling, p. 106).

Wait until the clock has completely wound down.

With the clock stopped, remove the hood (on hooded wall clocks and longcase clocks). Sometimes, inside the case, just below the bottom of the hood, a hidden swivelling catch or a vertical bolt locks the hood. Once this is undone the hood should slide forward; or sometimes on early English clocks the hood rises and may be held up by a catch on the back-board.

Lift the weights off their pulleys.

Stabilize the movement, with one hand on the edge of the dial, as it may not be secured in the case, and lift the pendulum up and back, off the suspension block, allowing the thin, delicate suspension spring to pass down through the crutch while lowering the pendulum (fig. 22). This operation is more easily performed with a helper (also wearing cotton gloves) at hand to stabilize the movement.

While the pendulum is out, be careful not to damage the suspension spring.

The movements of wooden-cased clocks can now be removed from the case. With 'tavern' clocks and the like, the movement can be left in.

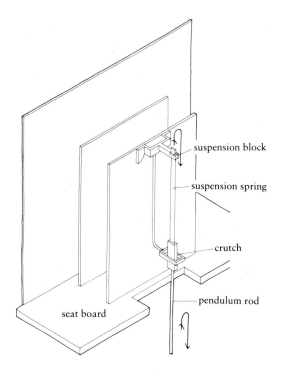

suspension block

suspension spring

crutch

pendulum rod

seat board

Fig. 22

The movements of eight-day and month-going clocks should be removed from the case with the seatboard, at the same time guiding the weight lines out of the case. This might mean unscrewing the seatboard, if it is not loose or, if it is firmly secured to the case with nails, seek the advice of a recommended clock-maker as the lines will have to be cut.

On thirty-hour clocks it is often possible simply to lift the movement out, guiding its rope or chain without having to remove the seatboard.

Clocks without cases, such as lantern clocks, can, of course, just be lifted down from the wall at this stage.

When the movement is down, the lines should be carefully wrapped around the seatboard, or coiled up neatly, to prevent them from becoming tangled with the movement or each other. Then it should be stored in a box padded with acid-free tissue paper.

The case can now be moved.

Setting up

To set up again, weight-driven clocks like longcase and hooded wall clocks should be screwed on to the wall, and this should only be done in consultation with the qualified clock-maker. Make sure that the case is vertical, not tilting forward or backward, so that the pendulum will be free to swing in the case.

Unwind the lines/rope/chain, and feed them into the case as you replace the movement. Here again, a helping hand is an advantage. Stabilize the movement until the weights are replaced.

Make sure the movement is central in the case; if it is too far back the crutch will touch the backboard. Rescrew the seatboard if applicable.

Find the bottom of each line with its pulley and hang the weight on the pulley stirrup or hook, at the same time making sure that the line is on the pulley wheel (fig. 23). Once this is done the timekeeping side of the clock might start to 'trip' - run faster than usual. This is quite normal.

Hang the pendulum on by carefully feeding the suspension spring up through the crutch and sliding the spring forwards through the fine slot in the middle of the suspension block (fig. 22).

Ideally the clock should be 'in beat' which means that the times between 'tick' and 'tock' should be equal. If necessary, this can be achieved by gently bending the crutch in the middle, but this is a delicate operation and if in any doubt (and the adjustment is only very slight), it is probably better to tilt the

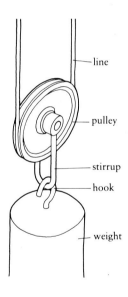

line

pulley

stirrup

hook

weight

Fig. 23

case very slightly. With longcase clocks, if the case is screwed to the wall it is often possible to shift the base of the clock sideways a little to bring the clock into beat.

These notes on handling are by necessity very brief, and there will inevitably be many exceptions to all these general rules. Therefore, if in any doubt always seek the advice of the recommended clock-maker.

15. The giant longcase clock by George Graham in the hall at Dunham Massey

16. The rare wooden mechanism from the longcase clock by John Harrison of Barrow, dated 1717, at Nostell Priory

STORING

Clocks in store must have their pendulums, weights, keys and other appendages clearly labelled and boxed, or attached to the clock in some way.

Watches not on display should be kept together, wrapped in acid-free tissue paper and locked up in a safe place.

Storage conditions, like display conditions, should avoid extremes of temperature and humidity, so areas such as cellars and attics should not normally be used.

A servant with this clause
Makes drudgery divine;
Who sweeps a room as for Thy laws
Makes that and th'action fine

George Herbert, 'The Elixir'
from The Temple, 1633

FLOORS

17. Hoogstraeten's *trompe-l'oeil* painting at Dyrham, dated 1662, showing a newly swept floor

FLOORS

INTRODUCTION

In the seventeenth and eighteenth centuries, floors seem to have been seldom polished. An American visitor to England in 1772 described them being 'washed and rubbed almost daily', so that they 'have a whitish appearance, and an air of freshness and cleanliness, which the finest inlaid floor has not always'. Small beer was sometimes used to scrub floors, and so was vinegar. But washing, because it made a room damp and could damage pieces of furniture and skirtings, was not as popular in practice as 'dry scrubbing'. Susannah Whatman's manuscript housekeeping book of 1776 advises the use of 'as little soap as possible (if any) in scowring rooms, Fuller's earth and fine sand preserves the colour of the boards, and does not leave a white appearance as soap does. All the rooms to be dry scrubbed with white sand.'

Hannah Glass, in her *Servants Directory*, published in 1760, also recommends this method: 'take some sand, pretty damp, but not too wet, and strew all over the Room, throwing it out of your Hand hard, and it will fly about the Floor and lick up all the Dust and Flew ... Sope is not proper for boards, and sand and water shews the grain, which is the beauty of a Board.' An alternative was to sweep the floor with herbs: 'Take tanzy, mint, and Balm; first sweep the Room, then strew the Herbs on the Floor, and with a long hard Brush rub them well all over the Boards, till you have scrubb'd the Floor clean. When the Boards are quite dry, sweep off the greens, and with a dry Rubbing brush dry-rub them well, and they will look like mahogany, of a fine brown, and never want any other washing, and give a sweet smell to the Room.'

Without a large labour-force at hand to clear a room of furniture and to wash or dry-rub floors almost daily, it is hardly practicable to employ such methods today, particularly in houses open to the public, where floors generally need the protection of polish. On the other hand, it should never be forgotten that the dry, silvery look of old boards (in a room like the Saloon at Uppark) is infinitely preferable to the high polish too often seen in eighteenth-century interiors today.

DUST PREVENTION

Housekeeping starts at floor level. Carpets and rugs take an incredible amount of wear and must be given protection from dust and grit, which abrade and cut the fibres (see Carpets and rugs, p. 200). Experiments by the International Wool Secretariat prove that people's shoes are only cleaned of normal dirt after walking over 3 m (3 yd) of absorbent matting.

Grids

Many paths and drives are surfaced with gravel which can scratch and cut into all types of floors. Metal or rubber grids set outside the entrance door can help clear stones from shoes.

Coconut matting

The lowly doormat is very important. In fact it is the first line of defence in keeping dust out of the house. Mats intended to clean visitors' feet should be at least large enough for both feet to fall on the mat when taking a normal stride. Large mats are heavy and difficult to handle so it is better to place two smaller mats together. Local ironmongers or builders' merchants will normally order special sizes from suppliers.

Coconut matting *must* be kept clean. It is so effective that, if not kept clean, it will simply get choked up with dust and start recycling dirt round the house instead of collecting it.

Vacuum daily with the strongest suction and at least once a week take the mat outside, turn it upside-down and beat it. Even more effective, occasionally take it outside, roll it up top side out and tie it before beating it with a stick. Rolling it up forces the fibres apart and lets the dirt out. When there is no time to take the mat outside, turn it upside-down and let people walk over it for a day. It is surprising how much dirt falls out. Only do this on the least busy day as the mat moves easily when upside-down and so could be a hazard. Do *not* beat the mat against a wall as this damages the edges.

Dust mats

There are many types of dust mat on the market, and some are very effective. However they are not pretty, and are therefore difficult to fit into the setting of a historic house. Some firms hire mats or runners of wool and nylon to collect dust and absorb water. The service includes replacement every two weeks. These mats are good in passages; and runners put down temporarily inside the entrance door on really wet days give such good protection to the house that the utilitarian look can be accepted.

Plastic socks

No visitor should be allowed to walk round a house wearing stiletto heels or in other unsuitable footwear like gumboots. Plastic socks are now available at such minimal cost that they can be given away. The socks stretch to fit most feet, and have been tried out and found not to be slippery.

In houses which have connoisseurs' days, where visitors are allowed to walk on certain carpets or delicate floors which would normally be protected by ropes, all visitors should wear plastic socks.

CARPETS AND RUGS

See Chapter 14, pp. 197 ff.

CLEANING

Dusting floors

Old stone floors which are beginning to break up are particularly dusty. To prevent dust from flying about, vacuum wood, stone, marble or tiled floors with an Electrolux 350E or, in large houses, with an industrial vacuum at low power. A dry mop picks up dust, but care must be taken to keep it clean.

Protect furniture from knocks by sticking a piece of thick art felt round the edges of the vacuum head.

Take great care that fringes on carpets, hangings and furniture are not sucked into the machine.

18. Plastic protective throw-away socks and overshoes

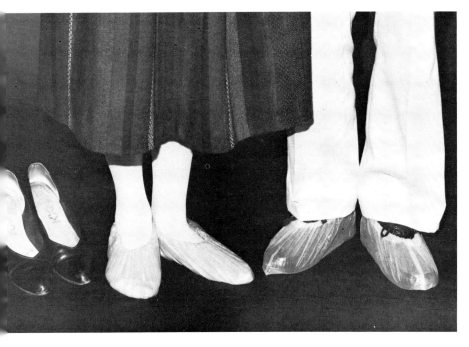

Scrubbing floors

Wash and scrub floors only when necessary. Add a little Synperonic N (see Appendix 3, p. 250) to warm water. Always use as little water as possible, rinse in clear water and dry quickly. Two buckets are needed.

All curtains and hangings should be lifted on to a windowsill or chair before any scrubbing or polishing is started.

Unpolished wood floors

Mop occasionally in clear water and dry off with a dry mop. If the floor has to be scrubbed, the scrubbing brush should not be too wet as water softens the wood. Scrub in the direction of the grain of the wood and not too vigorously.

Stone, marble or tiled floors

If soaked or left wet too long, harmful salts are activated, particularly in stone and marble, and the surface is damaged.

Furniture on stone, marble or tile floors often has a white tide-mark on the feet or base. This usually happens when too much water is used on the floor and it is left wet.

A scrubbing machine splashes, so place a piece of hardboard or 3-ply 45–60 cm (18–24 in) high and 1–1.2 m (3–4 ft) long against the skirting board. This prevents the walls from being marked. The more water used, the more the machine will splash. When scrubbing large areas a wet suction machine is almost essential for drying the floor quickly. Scrubbing and suction machines are very powerful and can cause damage to old stone and grouting, so use with care.

If the floor is of rough stone, a stiff brush can be used. First sprinkle damp sawdust to lay the dust.

Any black marks made by rubber heels on marble floors can be removed with a mixture of 0.3 l ($\frac{1}{2}$ pt) white spirit, 0.3 l ($\frac{1}{2}$ pt) water and a teaspoonful of Fairy Liquid. Shake well before and during use. Apply with small swabs of cotton wool, well squeezed out, and then rinse off in clear water before drying.

Polishing floors

Lift all curtains and hangings on to a windowsill or chair before any polishing is started. Also protect all edges of carpets.

Wood

A dry polish with the polisher is generally all that is needed, but make sure

19. The Little Parlour at Uppark. Wooden floors were often scrubbed or 'dry-rubbed' in the eighteenth century, rather than being polished

the brushes are clean. Never let a brush become impregnated with polish so that the bristles appear to have match-stick ends, because the brushes are then useless. To clean the brushes, soak the bristles in white spirit to soften the hardened polish and then wash and dry thoroughly before use.

A cloth impregnated with paraffin and vinegar is excellent since it collects the dust effectively and leaves the polished floor shiny. Tie the cloth round the head of a dry mop. To prepare impregnated cloths for floors, cut old woollen blankets into 60cm (24in) squares; soak in a 50/50 mixture of paraffin and malt vinegar; hang them out to dry and keep, when not in use, in screw-top jars or airtight plastic bags; 0.3 l ($\frac{1}{2}$pt) each of vinegar and paraffin is enough mixture for six cloths. Do not use man-made material as this dries out completely and is useless.

Very occasionally apply a little Johnson's Traffic Wax. The liquid form is easy to apply but do not use it more than two or three times a year or you will give yourself a lot of unnecessary work, and the polish will build up and become smeary so that every footmark and scuff will show. Too much polish will also darken the floor. Use a piece of hardboard to protect the skirting board from polish and marks from the polisher.

20. Watering the rush matting in the Long Gallery at Montacute

Stone and marble

Some houses have a tradition of polishing stone floors. But polish can radically change the colour and character of the floor and is difficult to remove. It is better to use dry mops, or dry polish with the polisher, using clean felt pads.

SEALING FLOORS

All seals change the character and colouring of the floor. Do not use them unless the dust problem is insupportable, and then try small sample areas before any seal is applied to the floor generally.

RUSH MATTING

To give this type of floor-covering some resilience it should be watered occasionally. Use a watering can fitted with a 45 cm (18 in) weedkiller bar (fine spray) to give a light covering; 4.5 l (1 gal) damps about 165 sq m (200 sq yd). When the rush matting is on wood floors in dry houses, this can be done two or three times a week. On stone floors and in damp conditions the matting should be watered less often, for there is danger that mould may grow under the matting.

If possible roll the matting up and vacuum the dust from underneath two or three times a year.

WOVEN COIR MATTING

This is very coarse and can mark wooden floors, which must therefore always be protected with carpet paper. When in use, the matting will stretch, but it can be shrunk back to size with a light watering (see above, Rush matting). Woven coir matting needs vacuuming very frequently.

COMPOSITION FLOORS – LINOLEUM, VINYL

Follow manufacturers' recommendations.

CHEWING-GUM

Rub chewing-gum with a block of ice until it gets so cold that it will just chip off.

Joint-stools were then created; on three legs
Upborne they stood. Three legs upholding firm
A massy slab, in fashion square or round.
On such a stool immortal Alfred sat,
And sway'd the sceptre of his infant realms:
And such in ancient halls and mansions drear
May still be seen; but perforated sore,
And drill'd in holes, the solid oak is found,
By worms voracious eating through and through.

William Cowper, from *The Task*, Book I,
'The Sofa', 1785

CHAPTER SIX

FURNITURE

21 and 22. The Cartoon Gallery at Knole, with its seventeenth-century seat furniture and (below) the famous Knole settee in the Leicester Gallery. Handling pieces of such rarity requires considerable expertise

·✤ FURNITURE ✤·

As a general rule, antique furniture should be moved and handled as little as possible.

It should always be carried using the lowest load-bearing member as a purchase. Moving even quite a small piece in this way usually needs two people. Even if it is fitted with castors, never drag a piece of furniture, however smooth the floor; it always puts a strain on the carcase and this can loosen the joints or even snap off a leg. It can also mark the floors badly.

Separate the object into smaller units where practicable before moving it, but if drawers are left in, lock them, and shut doors firmly so that they cannot fall open and be damaged while the object is being moved. If there is no key, tie wide tape right round the piece.

Before lifting the object, make sure that all parts to be handled are in sound condition. If furniture has to be turned over, it should be lifted up, turned in the air and put down squarely – if it is just tipped back, more weight is put on the back supports than they were intended to carry and they may well break under the strain.

All the legs and/or supports of furniture should share its weight; it is sometimes necessary to use wedges to compensate for an uneven floor or in cases where some legs are on a carpet and some are not.

Keep an eye on heavily loaded furniture and pieces with marble tops: if the stand is not in a sound condition it could be dangerous. The weight on top often makes an object appear more stable than it is. If a lot of furniture needs to be moved it is better to use trained furniture removers. Willing helpers in a country house, and particularly film crews, usually have no idea how to touch an object, let alone move it; they can also be difficult to control.

Seat furniture

Never touch original upholstery, where it survives, in the course of moving the piece of furniture. Deep fringes on seventeenth-century stools and chairs have suffered badly because the piece has been lifted by the seat rail.

Stools and chairs should be carried by the legs, particularly if the seats are covered in textiles or have fringes. This means that most chairs will need to be carried by two people.

Upholstered drop-in seats often break the seat rail joints when they are forced in. This is usually because a new cover has been put on top of the old one, making the seat too big.

In houses open to the public, no chairs of any historical value (particularly those belonging to sets) should be used by room attendants.

Drawers

Check that the drawers are not overloaded, and if a drawer is sticking, do not force it. Rubbing a white candle along the runners of the drawer will help it run smoothly.

Always pull on both drawer handles, where they exist. Do not force a drawer inwards, as it may knock off the back board of the chest or damage lip-mouldings on the drawer face.

Door catches

On bookcases, wardrobes and presses, ensure that interior catches are locked before closing the second door.

Mirrors

If a mirror with an elaborately carved frame has to be moved from the wall for any length of time, two lengths of batten should be screwed to the back, like legs, so that it can be stood vertically, without the frame touching the ground. Glass is very heavy and its weight can break the bottom of a carved frame, which was not made to carry it.

If such a mirror needs to be taken down in order to check for woodworm or to clean the back, it should be held off the floor by two people during this operation so that the weight is not on the carving.

Marble and glass tops

Never carry marble and glass tops flat, as they can break under their own weight. They should be raised into a vertical position and then lifted and carried vertically.

Handles

It is unwise ever to trust a handle, even if it has apparently been provided for the purpose of lifting.

Keys

In houses open to the public, keys should not be left in locks, since they may be pilfered. It is best to leave most pieces of furniture unlocked, since a determined thief will use a lever or hammer and damage a locked drawer or door. But it is better to secure all drawers and doors along the visitors' route in a house open to the public. Constant opening and shutting of drawers by the inquisitive puts a strain on handles, catches and hinges.

CLEANING

Polished wood surfaces – day-to-day care

The surface finish given to a piece of furniture when it was made was intended to be permanent; in normal circumstances it only needs a light dusting with a clean, dry duster to keep it clean and free of dust. Occasionally buff up the polished surface with a duster or chamois leather, which should be soft, clean and dry. Wax polish should only be used once or at most twice a year.

Care should be taken to collect the dust and not just to move it on. *Always* use a clean duster, which must be shaken out and washed regularly. (This obviously means that a good supply of dusters is needed.) Chamois leathers must also be kept very clean (see Appendix 3, Care of chamois leather, p. 250).

Never use dusters with raw edges and dangling threads, which can catch on the furniture, leaving tufts and even pulling pieces off.

Never use feather dusters as they cannot be washed and the feathers break and scratch the surface.

Be particularly careful when dusting furniture which has pieces of moulding or veneer missing because the pieces next to the gap are nearly always loose and could be knocked off.

Care should be taken that furniture, after day-to-day dusting, is put back in the right position. It is very easy for chairs to get pushed against walls, hangings and tapestries. Tables should stand clear of upholstered furniture and not, for example, rub against the backs of sofas.

Furniture in rooms with stone floors

Avoid the legs and bases of furniture when mopping stone floors. Furniture in rooms with stone floors needs very careful dusting to prevent white cement-like dust accumulating in the crevices.

Ornaments, flowers and jardinières

Put a piece of brown felt or chamois leather under ornaments to prevent their scratching the polished surface. Avoid brightly coloured felt because the colour could migrate on to the objects.

Flowers or plants standing on furniture must be very carefully watered, using a long-nosed can, not an ordinary jug, so as to avoid spillage and subsequent water stains. Keep flowers well away from gilded surfaces, which can be irreparably damaged by water. All vases must stand on a mat.

Avoid flowering plants which drip nectar on to polished surfaces. Take care that the wet leaves of plants do not touch the wood, because this results in water marks which cause staining, and damp can loosen the veneer.

Polished wood surfaces – spring-cleaning

Dusting

The result of spring-cleaning should be that objects look cared for without any obvious changes in their appearance; an object in a room may look shabby but it should look clean.

Time saved in not polishing unless really necessary should be spent in dusting thoroughly all the hidden places which there is not time to reach in day-to-day cleaning.

Thorough dusting, underneath a piece of furniture, round the back, inside and outside the drawers, so that every surface which can be reached is free of dust, is the greatest aid to conservation and the most important part of spring-cleaning. Wherever possible, all furniture should be moved once a year so that dust does not become trapped underneath and behind it and become a haven for moth and beetle.

Polishing

Never polish too near any pieces of wood that are cracking or lifting; if wax gets under them, it will make it more difficult to repair the furniture and glue back the bits.

Polish does not penetrate the surface and feed the wood, as is generally supposed; it gives the surface protection, an attractive appearance and a shiny finish, which is easier to dust than a dull one.

It is because wax polish builds up a protective surface over many years that it should always be applied very sparingly and evenly, and rubbed well in until a good shine has been built up. If the wax polish is put on too thickly the solvent in the polish evaporates before you have finished polishing, leaving the surface smeary and you will give yourself unnecessarily hard work trying to remove the smears on the surface with elbow grease.

USE ONLY THE RECOMMENDED WAX POLISH (see Appendix 4, p. 255). If the dye in the wax polish is darker than the object being treated it will darken the wood. If using lighter coloured polish on dark furniture, take care that no residue is left in the crevices, because it will show up when the wax dries out.

Furniture cream is not recommended because in order to keep the wax and solvent in suspension an emulsifying agent has to be used. Although many of these agents are harmless it is unfortunately impossible to check all the many cream polishes on the market, so it is better not to use them.

Never be tempted to use an aerosol polish, or any polish with silicone in it. These modern patent furniture polishes give an instant shine but there are several objections to their use: the film does not fill scratches and other surface blemishes, as wax does; with aerosol sprays the solvent comes out with such force that it can damage the polished surface; it can also make the surface dangerously slippery.

Where an aerosol is sprayed on frequently, the surface can acquire a slight milky look. No remedy has yet been found. It is IMPOSSIBLE to remove this aesthetically objectionable film without first stripping and then resurfacing the object.

Polished carved furniture

Occasionally it may be necessary to go over polished carved furniture with a soft bristle brush to remove dust trapped in the carving. Use a hogshair fitch brush. Never use the same brush on gilded surfaces, as wax must not get on the gilding.

On carved polished furniture, wax polish may be more easily applied and burnished with a soft bristle shoe brush.

Textiles

When polishing furniture, great care must be taken not to touch any of the textiles. Squab cushions and drop-in seats should be removed before polishing the woodwork. Take special care not to touch fringes.

Leather upholstery

To spring-clean plain leather upholstery, dust carefully and then apply Connolly's Hide Food with swabs of cotton wool. Use sparingly. Leave for twenty-four hours so that it will be absorbed well. Polish with a soft clean duster. If the leather upholstery has a badly damaged surface, do not treat it, but seek advice from an expert conservator.

Leather on desk-tops and bureau-falls can be similarly treated, avoiding any embossed gilding and taking care not to touch the surrounding wood.

Special cleaning of neglected polished woods

This is best undertaken with the advice of a furniture conservator, since these objects may well be in need of repair.

Where the piece is polished and the surface is sound, it is possible for the dirty surface to be washed, but only attempt small manageable areas at any one time. Reviving or resurfacing can only be carried out by the conservator. It may be necessary to wash furniture during spring-cleaning, especially if the house is very dusty or where visitors unavoidably touch certain pieces. You will need at least three cloths and two bowls. Put warm water in both bowls. Add a very little Synperonic N (see Appendix 3, p. 250) to one of the bowls of water. *Never* use commercial detergents, whether in powder or liquid form; they contain impurities, such as bleach, which can damage the surface. Use one cloth, well wrung out, for wiping the surface with the detergent; rinse off with water with the second cloth, well squeezed out. Then dry the surface immediately with the third cloth, which will have to be changed as soon as it gets at all damp. Leave the object overnight, until thoroughly dry, before applying a thin coat of wax polish in the usual way.

Never let water get near any gilded surface.

Brass fittings

When the furniture was made, the wood was bright and unfaded so that bright, brass handles (sometimes gilded) acted as a complement to it. Now the wood has faded, the brass should be allowed to tone down with it. This also applies to metal inlays.

Where there are brass fittings on furniture, such as handles or knobs, the patina on the surface of the brass should *never* be removed. The brass should look cared for but not gleaming or shiny. To get this effect, brass should only be polished at the same time as the wood, using the same wax furniture polish.

Never use a patent brass cleaner on brass fittings on furniture. As well as making the brass too bright, it also often leaves a smear and white marks on the wood round the brass. Removal of smears on the wood round handles and mounts where a patent metal cleaner has been used in the past is best left to a furniture conservator.

Day-to-day cleaning should be exactly the same as for the rest of the piece of furniture: ordinary dusting, and an occasional buff-up with a clean, dry chamois leather or duster.

Boulle, tortoiseshell, lacquered, japanned and papier mâché surfaces, painted furniture

The metal marquetry of Boulle is nearly always slightly loose and higher than the tortoiseshell, so rubbing over the surface with a cloth or chamois would catch in the metal and pull it out.

Never use a duster. If the surface is sound, brush Boulle with a soft banister brush or blow rather than dust the surface, using the blow action of the Electrolux 350E. Boulle should never be polished.

If lacquer is flaking or crumbling, it should be left alone, because this indicates deep-seated disturbance for which treatment is difficult. A furniture conservator will advise on day-to-day maintenance of damaged pieces as this will vary according to the extent of the damage. This also applies to the other categories mentioned above.

23. Detail of a Boulle bureau at Erddig, showing the lifting of the brass and tortoiseshell marquetry

Gilded furniture

If any piece of gilt or gesso seems to be flaking, the object should not be cleaned; advice should be sought from a furniture conservator.

Never rub gilding; if it is necessary to brush the dust out of the carving on gilded furniture use a ponyhair fitch brush and brush off the dust into a Hoover Dustette held in the other hand. Take care not to knock the gilded surface.

Never let water get on any gilded surface as it could ruin it.

Never touch in gilding with any form of gold paint because it gives a totally different effect and will discolour anyway.

Glazing

If the glass is not very dirty, just buff it up with a dry chamois leather or soft lintless duster, taking care not to rub any gilded edges round the glass.

If the panes of glass on a piece of furniture such as a glazed bookcase are very dirty, dust them and then wipe the glass over with methylated spirits on cotton-wool swabs. Use the swabs when they are almost dry and with a circular motion so as to avoid leaving streaks. Keep changing the swabs as soon as they are dirty.

The swabs must not be allowed to touch polished wood surfaces or gilding. Hold a postcard against the inside edge so that the swab is kept away from the surrounding wood.

Card tables

The felt on card tables can become a haven for moths, so vacuum carefully with the Hoover Dustette at least once a year.

FURNITURE IN NEED OF REPAIR

While cleaning look out for damage such as lifting veneers or brass inlay and flaking lacquer, or structural defects such as rickety legs.

Never attempt to stick bits back on the furniture. Any bits should be carefully stored in a bit box and left to the furniture conservator to replace. The sealed plastic bags in which bits are kept should be clearly marked to identify the piece of furniture, its inventory number, location in the house and, if possible, the position of the damage and the date the damage was discovered.

WOODWORM OR FURNITURE BEETLE

Woodworm is a widespread and potentially very serious problem; it has been found to be active in practically every National Trust house.

Woodworm infestation is usually found in glue blocks inside furniture, inside seat rails, in the blocks of tip-up tables, in hinged brackets under table flaps, in drawer linings, and generally in parts of furniture which are more functional than decorative. It is also found in old oak furniture or the sapwood of oak, and anywhere in furniture made of walnut, pine, beech, ash and various other woods.

Life cycle

The eggs are laid in crevices and on rough surfaces of the wood, and hatch within four weeks. The grubs immediately begin to bore into the wood and will remain there for between one and five years. During this time the wood is being tunnelled and consequently weakened.

Inspection

A look-out must be kept at all times for signs of active woodworm, and a thorough inspection made once a year.

A torch should be used; if it is shone across a board of wood, any new flight-holes will be shown up quite clearly by the clean wood inside the hole and its sharp, freshly cut edge. This is more effective than looking for the little piles of frass or wood dust which appear on the surface of the wood or on the floor underneath, since these are often swept up before enough has accumulated to be noticed.

Always inspect a new piece of furniture for woodworm and treat it if necessary before admitting it to a house.

Treatment

Late spring and summer are the most effective times for treatment, when the beetles are emerging or eggs and newly hatched grubs are near the wood surface. Treatment should be given immediately signs of attack are noticed, but it may be impractical to treat the furniture while a house is open to the public, in which case it should be dealt with as soon as possible after the house closes in the autumn.

Work in a well-ventilated room or near an open window if possible, and wear rubber gloves, and goggles or glasses. If necessary, protect the floor with a polythene sheet.

Use a plastic injector bottle with an applicator or a special syringe (see Appendix 4, p. 255) to inject Cuprinol Woodworm Killer Low Odour into holes every 5 cm (2 in) or so. The fluid sometimes comes straight back out of another hole, hence the need to protect the eyes. Then use a paint-brush to apply fluid liberally to all unfinished surfaces (e.g. insides, backs, and undersides). If any fluid gets on to a 'finished' surface, it must be wiped off quickly and carefully.

If possible, treat an object in this way and then top up with fluid a couple more times within the next month to get really good penetration. Make a note of the piece of furniture. Repeat this treatment for at least two years running, and even after really thorough treatment do not give up the annual inspection. This is because woodworm infestation is often very persistent and it is rarely eradicated completely.

For the treatment to be effective, it may be necessary to separate furniture into its component parts and/or turn it upside-down (see Handling, p. 83). Take the opportunity to clean inside, underneath, etc. (see Dusting, p. 86).

Great care should be taken not to contaminate textiles with insecticide fluid when treating furniture for woodworm; where there is danger of this, it would be better to get an expert to treat the area.

LIGHT

Light affects the colour of wood. Light wood tends to get darker and dark wood tends to get lighter. Where the surface is made up of more than one

24 and 25. Woodworm damage: (above) to a fragment of limewood carving from Kingston Lacy; (below) on the frame of a walnut chair from Canons Ashby

wood, contrast can be lost, and thus the design. Damage caused by light cannot be reversed without removing some of the surface.

If daylight falls unevenly or only on part of a piece of furniture, the surface will acquire a patchy appearance. Move objects on a wood surface from time to time to prevent dark unfaded patches occurring.

Where textiles are part of the furniture, they will deteriorate rapidly if exposed to strong light. Sunlight must be prevented from falling on the textiles. Fit sun-blinds and use them.

HEAT

Avoid placing any radiant heaters near a piece of furniture, or placing furniture near a fire or radiator. Hot spotlights or lamps may equally affect the timber and polish.

STORAGE

Store-rooms should be kept clean as the contents are very vulnerable to attack by woodworm, moth, mould, etc.

A complete list of objects in store should be available and stored pieces should be inspected once a year and checked off on the list.

To avoid damage from rising damp and condensation, furniture should not be stored directly on a stone or brick floor, and also not too near outside walls. Proximity to damp walls can also affect furniture in rooms that are lived in, or open to the public; a 5 cm (2 in) gap behind every piece will allow the air to circulate freely. Basements are therefore unlikely to make suitable store-rooms.

Exclude light as far as possible by closing shutters or blacking out the windows, but remember that it is important to have adequate ventilation. Avoid sudden changes in temperature and humidity. Attics are only suitable if the roof is well insulated.

Cover stored objects with a dust-sheet to protect them from light and dirt (see Appendix 3, Dust-sheets, p. 250). Objects in store get scratched and damaged easily. Do not stack anything on top of a polished surface.

Dust-sheets must be washed so that dirty dust-sheets are not put on to the clean furniture. Covering the furniture with dust-sheets is particularly important when builders are working in the house. Care should be taken in placing and removing dust-sheets to avoid tearing off loose gilding and veneer.

SECURITY

Use nylon fishing line if, for security, small objects have to be tied down. Metal wire can damage both the object and the piece of furniture it is tied to. *Never* try to stick objects to the surface of any piece of furniture.

John Vavassour de Quentin Jones
Was very fond of throwing stones ...
Like many of the Upper Class
He liked the Sound of Broken Glass*
It bucked him up and made him gay
It was his favourite form of Play.

(*A line I stole with subtle daring
From Wing-Commander Maurice Baring.)

Hilaire Belloc,
Cautionary Tales for Children, 1907

GLASS

26. A late-seventeenth-century Bohemian glass goblet and cover at Waddesdon Manor

✣ GLASS ✣

Accidents and repairs

Broken pieces should be carefully wrapped in tissue paper, clearly labelled and put away safely. Repairs should only be attempted by an expert.

Handling

Glass is light and is easily knocked over. When glass has to be moved out of the way to reach something, place it on another surface near by and do not just push it to one side.

Glass is less easily seen than ceramics so do not leave glass near the edge of a table – it is liable to be brushed against or knocked over.

Never pick up a glass by using finger and thumb on the rim. Cup the bowl in one hand and where possible support the base with the other hand so as to cradle the glass from knocks.

Never try to carry more than one glass at a time unless you are using a basket or wire tray, and then make sure that the objects are well padded with tissue paper.

As with ceramics, never turn to talk to someone while putting a piece of glass down as it is easy to misjudge the distance of the base of the object from the table top. Set the base of the glass down flat and not heavily or at an angle.

Storing

As with ceramics, make sure the objects are thoroughly dry before they are put away.

Do not overcrowd shelves and *never* let glass objects touch each other. Place smaller items at the front so that they can be seen.

Never put glass objects one inside another.

Make sure there is sufficient clearance from the front of the shelves, so that the glass will not be squashed and broken when the doors are closed.

Spring-cleaning

Glass which has painted or gilded decoration or early glass (pre-1700) should not be touched. Decoration often adheres lightly and should be handled as little as possible. Consult an expert when necessary.

Preliminary examination

Examine the object carefully before washing.

Repairs

Never immerse glass which has been repaired. A water-soluble adhesive was commonly used to bond glass and the pieces will part company very easily. Repairs to the stem are often difficult to see. To clean repaired glass wipe cautiously with swabs of cotton wool, which should be damp rather than wet.

Metal and ormolu mounts

Metal, especially ormolu, must not get wet. Glass which has metal mounts should only be dusted or, if very dirty, the glass only cleaned with slightly damp swabs of cotton wool and dried immediately.

Washing

Use lukewarm water with a very little Synperonic N (see Appendix 3, p. 250); if you use too much, you will not be able to see the glass in the bowl because of the suds.

Never put more than one glass object at a time in the bowl and never leave anything in the bowl if you are called away. Someone could easily come along and drop something in which would cause a breakage.

Be careful not to put pressure on the rim of the bowl of the glass either from the inside or outside.

Draining and drying

Never put glass straight down on to a wet, smooth surface to drain. It could easily skid, especially if put down on its rim. Paper towels laid down on the surface are a good idea as they prevent slipping and also absorb the excess water as the glasses drain.

The slightest impact is enough to break glass so do not overcrowd the working surface. It is sometimes difficult to judge how much space you have between the objects.

Use a soft cloth or paper towel for drying, taking care not to put excess pressure on any one area, particularly the rim or bowl. Never hold a glass by the stem when drying as it could snap under pressure – support it by cupping one hand under the bowl.

CHANDELIERS

During the winter months the amount of dust and dirt that settles on chandeliers is considerably reduced if they are protected by muslin bags.

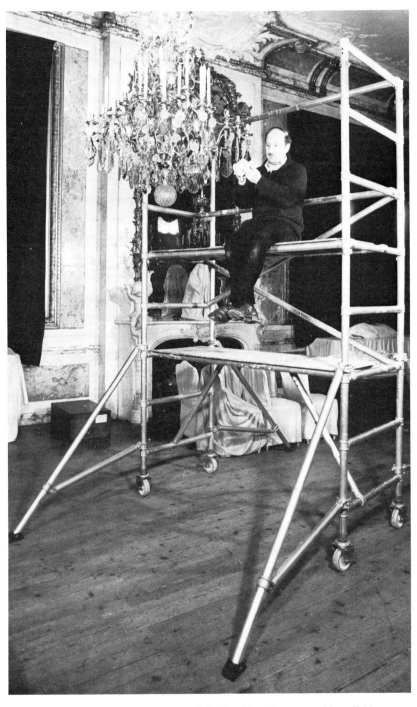

27. A steward at Waddesdon cleaning one of the chandeliers from a portable scaffold

28. A pair of large giltwood rococo pier glasses, *c.* 1755, at Uppark

Cleaning

Before dismantling a chandelier several black and white photographs should be taken so that there is a clear record of where each piece belongs. Colour photographs do not show up enough detail.

Have plenty of wicker baskets or strong cardboard boxes available in which to put the pieces as they are taken down.

As dismantling and cleaning is a major operation it would be wise to get the main chain and fixtures to the ceiling tested while the chandelier is down to ensure that there are no weaknesses.

Keep a record of when a chandelier is dismantled and checked.

Washing

Every piece should be examined for damage, and damaged pieces set aside so that they are not handled or washed carelessly.

As well as examining the glass itself, all the metal hooks and connections should be looked at for signs of weakness or corrosion and should be replaced by new ones where necessary.

The glass can be washed in lukewarm water to which a little Synperonic N has been added. (See Washing, p. 56, for the reasons why soap and household detergents should never be used.)

Drying

Make sure that every piece is dry before re-assembly, particularly the metal hooks and connections, as they could corrode. The most effective way of drying these is to use a hair-dryer, set at cold.

MIRRORS

Cleaning

Check how the mirror is fixed to the wall. If it is large it is safer for two people to be present for cleaning, so that one person can do any steadying that may be necessary.

Examine the frame before any cleaning is done. It is not easy to distinguish different types of gilding, so it is best to assume that it is water gilding which would come away if wiped with a damp cloth. A little methylated spirits on swabs of cotton wool is probably the safest method of cleaning the glass. Buff up with a clean, dry chamois leather, but avoid touching or rubbing the edges of the frame, as methylated spirits must not be allowed to touch oil gilding.

Do not use household window-cleaning preparations on mirrors.

For cleaning the frame, see Dusting frames, p. 154.

I would to God my name were not so terrible to the enemy as it is: I were better eaten to death with rust than to be scoured to nothing with perpetual motion.

Shakespeare, 2 *Henry IV*, 1600

CHAPTER EIGHT

METALWORK

29. Ambassadorial silver in the dining-room at Ickworth

·✤ METALWORK ✤·

It is a mistake to think that metals are hard and infinitely durable. Metal surfaces are easily scratched and worn away. Metalwork should be kept in dry conditions because most metals are naturally unstable in the atmosphere and tend to oxidize and corrode. This corrosion is greatly accelerated by the presence of moisture. It can be extremely rapid and can cause complete destruction of the object. Discuss any signs of corrosion or disfigurement such as white or green crystals or powders with a conservator.

Extreme caution should be taken when handling a very neglected object, however mundane it may appear to be. No work should be done without consulting an expert.

Never try to polish up a neglected piece with patent cleaners. Untold damage could be done to the surface and the patination could be entirely destroyed.

Patina

Patina is the surface coating of a metal object. It can be a natural result of the ageing process of the metal and therefore part of its history, or it may have been artificially applied. The patina is nearly always desirable. *Never* attempt to remove a patina without first consulting a metalwork conservator because the appearance of objects has sometimes been altered through the centuries to suit the tastes of the time. Occasionally preservatives have been applied, such as wax or oil, which have produced patinas. Sometimes objects have been painted as the easiest way of overcoming a conservation problem, perhaps to even out a blotchy appearance, e.g. the Le Sueur bust of Charles I at Stourhead, which was originally gilded and later painted. Lead statuary was frequently painted white to simulate marble or coloured to look like stone, and this has the added virtue of protecting the lead from the atmosphere. (See also Garden sculpture and ornaments, p. 185.)

Day-to-day care

Dusting of metal objects should be kept to a minimum because dust can be abrasive. *Never* rub when dusting, just flick the dust lightly off the surface with a hogshair brush. Do not use a feather duster because it cannot be washed; also the feathers break and then scratch the surface of the object. Where possible the dusting of metal should be limited to two or three times a year.

Never polish as part of day-to-day care. Any polishing, even with a dry duster, is abrasive and will eventually blunt and disfigure even the most apparently solid object. Constant polishing of, say, door handles and finger-plates will eventually mute and perhaps destroy the original decoration.

Where it is permissible to polish a metal object, cover the edge of the work table with something soft such as foam rubber or an old cushion or pillow, so that the object is not dented or scratched while it is being polished. But all polishing should be kept to an absolute minimum.

Handling

Once metalwork has been polished or lacquered *never* touch it with bare hands because acidity in the skin will tarnish the metal. *Always* wear cotton gloves and keep them clean by washing them fairly frequently.

Lacquering

Metalwork that has been lacquered need not be touched again for five or ten years, except for the minimum of light dusting. Surfaces that are easily abraded or destroyed through constant polishing should be treated first, such as collections of silver-gilt and Sheffield plate. The National Trust also envisages lacquering silver, brass and copper in due course.

Metalwork should only be lacquered by experts because the preparation of the item is complicated and must be left to a metal conservator.

It will help the conservator to decide on priorities if, when listing items to be lacquered, it is recorded whether the tarnish is very thick or a brown colour. This gives an indication of the degree of tarnishing and of the length of time the object has been tarnished.

When helping a conservator to prepare objects for lacquering always wear cotton gloves, because the natural oils and grease in the skin inhibit the lacquer from adhering to the surface of the metal.

When items have been lacquered, a record should be kept listing the inventory number and date of treatment, to ensure that the piece, once lacquered, is not then polished by mistake. The date is important because it gives some idea of when the item will need to be lacquered again.

GOLD

Never touch the surface of gold except to dust lightly with a clean, dry duster or chamois leather.

SILVER-GILT

Silver-gilt is silver with a covering of gold. *Never* polish or you will remove the gold, revealing the silver underneath, which will then tarnish in the atmosphere. Arrangements should be made for a metalwork conservator to lacquer silver-gilt objects.

Sheffield plate is a thin coating of silver on a copper base. *Never* rub the surface by polishing, as this removes the silver, revealing the copper underneath. Just flick the dust off with a soft duster when absolutely necessary.

Never replate. When the piece was made sterling silver would have been used which has some copper in it, but modern electrolytic techniques would deposit pure silver on the surface and so alter the appearance of the piece.

Electroplating has been in use as a manufacturing technique since 1840. The coating of silver is even thinner than that on Sheffield plate and the base metal can be a silvery-coloured alloy which makes it difficult to see when the silver layer has been polished away.

SILVER

Never use plate powder for cleaning; it is advisable to use Goddard's Silver Dip or Long Term Silver Foam. Goddard's Long Term could inhibit lacquering at a later stage.

Arrangements should be made to lacquer silver not in use. In the meantime clean it using the procedure outlined in the following paragraphs.

Plain (untooled) silver – cleaning

Lightly tarnished silver

Wash in warm water to which a little Synperonic N has been added. Dry thoroughly with mutton cloth, paper towels, or old, soft, linen tea towels. Do not dry with new dressed linen tea cloths because they are too abrasive. When thoroughly dry, polish with Goddard's Long Term Silver Cloth.

Heavily tarnished silver

Use only Goddard's Silver Dip. Apply with cotton-wool swabs, following the manufacturer's directions. Rinse off under running water very thoroughly. Dry with mutton cloth and then polish with Goddard's Long Term Silver Cloth. When dealing with a large object, clean a small area at a time, rinsing off the Silver Dip before going on to clean the next area.

Silver Dip should not be re-used indefinitely because it becomes over-charged with silver which gets deposited back on the surface as matt silver. Pour a fresh lot out from time to time and never dip anything into your main supply.

30. The Countess of Stamford's toilet-service, by Magdalen Feline, 1754, at Dunham Massey

Tooled silver – cleaning

Small objects

Use only a soft brush specially made for silver cleaning; do not use a toothbrush or household paint-brush, because their bristles will scratch and abrade the surface. Be sure to use these brushes for silver *only*. Do not over-insist or you may abrade the tops of the tooling leaving the valleys undisturbed. Where necessary take a wooden cuticle-stick with cotton wool wrapped round the end. Dip it in Silver Dip, work gently into crevices to remove tarnish, and rinse well.

Large objects

Use a plate brush (see Appendix 4, p. 253) to get into the grooves of the tooling; the correct type of bristle and the degree of stiffness are important. Consult a conservator when in doubt.

Storing silver

If it has not been lacquered, silver which is to be stored should be wrapped in plenty of acid-free tissue paper to exclude the air because hydrogen sulphide in the atmosphere tarnishes silver.

Do not use baize, felt or chamois leather for wrapping silver as these give off hydrogen sulphide, which is the active blackening tarnishing agent in the atmosphere. Do not wrap silver in cling-wrap or use plastic bags, because condensation can form inside the covering.

Silver which has been lacquered can be stored without any special protection provided that there is enough space on the shelf to avoid the danger of scratching the surface of one object against another.

BRONZE

The treatment of bronze is specialized and difficult. *Never* try and clean bronze statues or statuettes. There are many types of patination, including over-painting, some of which could easily come off, revealing flaws or repairs.

Never wash bronze because this could cause rapid corrosion promoted by the presence of chlorides (bronze disease). If this were to happen it would involve complicated restoration and complete repatination of the surface. Furthermore the disease could keep recurring.

Never use water or methylated spirits on bronze.

The surface of bronze should not be touched except once or twice a year when it can be dusted lightly. Dust is abrasive so do not rub the surface when dusting.

Once a year remove carefully the dust trapped in the tooling of the bronze with a soft bristle brush. This is important because the dust lying in the grooves can act like a sponge and attract moisture, which could cause bronze disease.

Do not keep brushing away at the tops of the tooling. When necessary take a wooden cuticle-stick with clean *dry* cotton-wool wrapped round the end and carefully remove the dust from crevices.

Never touch neglected bronze yourself, because only after careful tests is it possible to know how the patina was formed.

PEWTER

It is often preferable to leave the dull grey patination on pewter. *Never* do more than dust it with a soft dry cloth or chamois leather.

Keep a look-out for pewter disease. This is a white powdery substance appearing on the surface of the pewter which sometimes leads to flaking and

31. Gilt-bronze door furniture, designed by Robert Adam, in the Saloon at Saltram

peeling of small areas of metal. Report any signs at once to a metal conservator.

If the environment of pewter is to be changed either by putting it into a showcase or by decorating the room, the object could become unstable through bringing it into contact with some form of acidity. Pewter should be kept out of rooms while they are being decorated and should never be in direct contact with untreated, unseasoned wood. While an oak dresser is the traditional place for displaying pewter, serious deterioration can be caused by organic acids from the oak. Pewter can be displayed on an oak surface provided there is plenty of air circulating around it, but *never* put pewter away in a drawer or cupboard made of oak.

ORMOLU

The gold-coloured mounts on furniture, clocks and candelabra are made of bronze or brass coated with a thin layer of gold. This is true ormolu, and the gold coat is as vulnerable as the gold layer on silver-gilt, or the silver layer on Sheffield plate.

Mounts that look like ormolu may be of brass coated with coloured lacquer.

The base metal of some gilded pieces may not be bronze but the more brittle zinc (spelter), and this can easily fracture. The gilding on zinc is also less securely attached.

Never wash, rub or polish ormolu, whether true or imitation. Dust lightly and only once or twice a year.

If ormolu candlesticks are used, protect them with candle grease catchers, small circles of plastic or glass placed on top of the candle holder. If candle grease gets on to ormolu, it can be softened with methylated or white spirit. On no account use anything hard or abrasive to remove the grease from the gilded surface.

BRASS AND COPPER

Although much of this ware is domestic and utilitarian, some of it has beautifully chased or etched decoration which would be worn away by constant polishing. This applies particularly to door furniture.

Lacquering should be envisaged for the more important pieces; in the meantime clean only when necessary, as follows:

32. The kitchen at Hardwick with its copper *batterie de cuisine*

Lightly tarnished

Rub with Goddard's Long Term Silver Cloth. Brass and copper should each have their own cloths, and *never* use either of these cloths on silver.

Heavily tarnished

Use Solvol Autosol, which is only mildly abrasive. It is available in tubes, which have a long shelf life, even when opened, provided the tops are replaced.

Apply with pads of cotton wool. Burnish with a soft clean cloth. A plate brush is useful for getting the polish out of cracks and corners. Keep one brush for brass and another for copper.

If copper pots are standing on a stone floor, isolate them from the stone with wooden slats or mats, as damp from the floor can corrode the metal.

As a matter of policy brass fittings on furniture such as handles or knobs should not be polished. The brass should look cared for but not gleaming or shiny. To get this effect brass on furniture needs no special polishing (see Brass fittings, p. 88).

STEEL GRATES, FIREPLACES, FIRE-IRONS

It may be difficult to distinguish the raised decorations and use of materials when they are obscured by dirt and rust. A metal conservator would make careful cleaning tests.

Gilding and engraving on steel

An object in steel should be checked carefully to see whether there is any gilding or engraving. When a piece is dirty or rusty, gilding is often only discernible by an expert, who can test likely areas before work is begun. For example, in Adam-type fireplaces some of the embellishments may be in gilt-bronze (often the lozenge-shaped decoration). Engraving would be rubbed out completely if emery paper were used to remove rust.

Blueing

The colouring of the metal is literally blue – in shades of dark blue through to peacock blue. This is difficult to distinguish under a layer of dirt. Where there is any doubt, do not touch until the next visit of a metal conservator except to wipe over with methylated spirits on cotton-wool swabs to remove the surface dirt. In order to help stabilize the surface and prevent any further deterioration, small quantities of Renaissance Wax can then be applied, but as it will have to be removed in order to carry out the necessary conservation, do not do so if a visit is imminent.

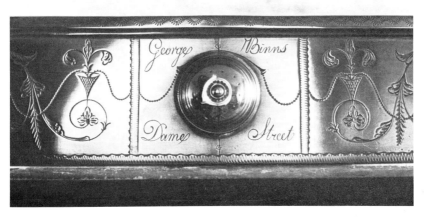

33 and 34. A polished steel grate and chimney-surround at Castle Coole and (below) a detail of the central inscription

Cleaning plain steel

Whether action can be taken without the help of a metal conservator depends on the degree of rust.

Steel with no rust

Clean with Solvol Autosol (Appendix 4). Apply with small swabs of cotton wool. Keep polishing in the same direction, using a lateral and not a circular motion. When polishing bars, go backwards and forwards along the bar, rather than round it. Care should be taken not to get a build-up of white powder in cracks and corners. A plate brush is useful for this. Keep one brush for steel only.

Steel affected by rust

Rust shows up in brown patches. It can be cleaned off with Solvol Autosol and fine wire-wool, grade ooo or oooo. Any coarser grade will make scratches on the surface, leaving untouched valleys in between and, as well as damaging the surface, it will take far more work before you get a smooth unblemished finish.

Very rusted steel

Heavy rust which has eaten into the surface should be left alone until the amount of metal which is left can be checked by a metal conservator. Iron and steel can be completely eaten away in places.
   Never use a patent rust remover.
   Never use an electric or any other form of mechanical burnisher.
   Never use a wire brush on polished steel grates.

Dismantling

No attempt should be made to dismantle a fireplace, or other object, without first consulting a metal conservator in order that the necessary precautions may be taken.

Grates

If black lead is already being used, continue to use it. Black lead is available in tubes (Zebrite). An alternative, if the grate is not in use, is to paint it with International matt black paint or Manders Black Ebony paint, finish M.757. Apply only a very thin coat; a thick coat of paint would change the appearance of the grate and obliterate decoration and evidence of natural wear which is all part of the history of the grate. Thin the paint, if necessary, with a little white spirit.

KITCHEN RANGES (CAST IRON)

When rusty, brush over the surface with a wire brush. Use a bristle brush to remove any loose dirt or dust. Wipe over the surface with methylated spirits on cotton-wool swabs. *Never* use water. If not in use paint with a thin coat of International matt black paint or Manders Black Ebony paint, finish M.757, but first try a small area on a part that does not show and leave for about a week. The paint may peel off if the surface is unsuitable, so it is unwise to paint the whole thing until it is certain that the paint will adhere. If it does peel off, ask a metal conservator for another suggestion.

Never use a wire brush on any other object or metal surface.

ARMS AND ARMOUR

Arms, armour and swords should be looked at by a specialist metal conservator before they are touched. It is difficult to recognize the various metals and materials, let alone distinguish the decoration. Arms, armour and fire-arms could be blued, silvered, russetted, or have brass inlays. There may also remain traces of fine engraving. Inexpert cleaning, even wiping over with a dry duster, can lift and remove minute particles of valuable decoration.

Cleaning is best left to a metal conservator, as it depends on the amount and type of decoration. Arms and armour must be dismantled by an expert, or damage on the parts out of sight will be overlooked. For example, the barrel of a blunderbuss may be made of either steel or brass. It must be dismantled to be cleaned properly as the underside is inaccessible until the barrel is separated from the wooden stock. This also applies to the mechanical sections of the lock and other detachable embellishments. The construction of fire-arms varies according to period and type; a comprehensive knowledge of the history of a fire-arm is necessary to be able to ensure that no damage is done in handling it.

No fire-arm should be taken apart by an amateur, as it is important for the metal conservator to be able to see its general condition and how it is at present put together. He can then judge the degree of cleaning and conservation necessary.

Security can be a problem, as weapons are now popular and have increased in value during the last few years. Consult a metal conservator about how they should be exhibited and the correct type of supports. All fixing or hanging points for arms or armour should be protected by chamois leather or plastic tubing and any part of the armour or weapon that touches a wall should be insulated from it by means of a piece of cork.

If armour is kept in a room where there are signs of condensation, expert advice should be sought.

And that you may know how to shelter your Lute, in the worst of Ill weathers, (which is moist) you shall do well, ever when you Lay it by in the day-time, to put It into a Bed, that is constantly used, between The Rug and Blanket; but never between the Sheets, because they may be moist with Sweat, etc. . . . a Bed will . . . keep your Glew so Hard as Glass, and All safe and sure; only to be excepted, That no Person be so inconsiderate, as to Tumble down upon the Bed whilst the Lute is There; For I have known several Good Lutes spoil'd with such a Trick.

Thomas Mace, *Musick's Monument*, 1676

CHAPTER NINE

MUSICAL INSTRUMENTS

Introduction

Avoiding Accidents

Enemies and Snags

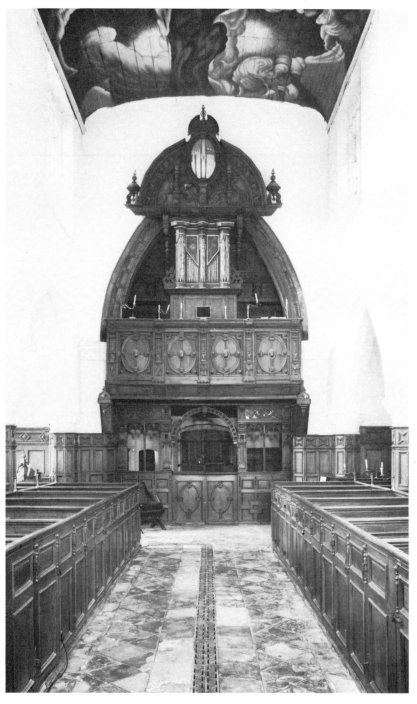

35. The seventeenth-century organ in the church at Staunton Harold

·✤ MUSICAL INSTRUMENTS ✤·

INTRODUCTION

The conservation of musical instruments depends on proper care being taken of the materials and adhesives used in their construction. Five factors make adherence to this obvious direction more difficult.

The variety of component materials

In most musical instruments a diversity of materials is to be found, many of them organic and therefore particularly susceptible to alterations in temperature and humidity as well as to attack by pests of various sorts. Different materials vary in their reaction to atmospheric change and this fact leads not only to obvious damage like loose Boulle work and to ivories becoming detached from their keylevers but also to problems of mechanical regulation. Instruments made largely of relatively stable materials often incorporate less stable parts of organic origin; the skin forming the head of a brass kettledrum is an obvious instance but not an isolated one. An ivory flute will have joints of cork or thread and key-pads of leather. A modern iron-framed grand piano will still have action parts of wood and garniture of leather and felt.

The delicate nature of the component parts

Parts of many musical instruments are of a size or thickness which renders them vulnerable. Some are manifestly fragile, like the elaborate roses of early guitars and of some harpsichords. Some are robust enough for their job but too delicate to mishandle, like return springs of hog's bristle or whalebone. The strength or weakness of other parts is not so obvious. Harpsichord soundboards can be less than 2 mm ($\frac{1}{12}$ in) thick in places and the tables of lutes, theorbos (a type of bass lute), guitars and similar instruments are often equally thin. Although their backs and ribs are usually of hardwood, they are almost as delicate and just as liable to damage.

Such thin material readily reacts to alterations in humidity. The problem is acute in the case of fronts and soundboards, which are commonly made of quarter-sawn softwood. Expansion and contraction is most marked in this dimension. General joinery practice allows such panels room for movement by loose-tongueing them into the rabbets of the surrounding frame. Such freedom of movement cannot be allowed to a soundboard since it would rattle and buzz when energized. It is therefore glued in position around its edge and can only react to high humidity by distorting and to low humidity by splitting.

Tension

Stringed instruments, with or without keyboards, are load-bearing structures. The modern grand piano supports an aggregate string tension of about twenty tons, more or less the weight of an empty railway carriage. Earlier examples of the piano and, obviously, other types of instrument with fewer strings, are not subjected to such considerable loading, but in all cases tension can both provoke and accentuate distortion.

Tolerances

The tolerances involved in the proper functioning of musical instruments are often very small. The thickness of tissue paper rather than that of a visiting card gives an idea of the distance between good and bad regulation. Moving parts must function freely but noiselessly. The difference between mechanical stiffness and audible action slop is measured in thousandths of an inch and provoked by relatively small variations in humidity. Similarly small movements can prevent the effective closure of organ pallets and impair the wind-tightness of oboes, bassoons and the like.

The domestic environment

The conservation of instruments in their domestic surroundings can subject them to conditions unavoidably inferior to those afforded by the controlled environment of a good museum or, for the smaller examples, a showcase. Physical and mechanical damage is more likely, dust and airborne pollution can present more of a problem, fluctuations in temperature and humidity are likely to be greater, attack by moth and worm is more probable. Sunlight has to be considered a threat, not only in its discolouring effects but also as a source of heat.

AVOIDING ACCIDENTS

Lids

Some harpsichords and pianos have loose-pin spine hinges to make lid-removal easier. Make sure the pins are in place before opening the lids of such instruments. Many lids are secured when shut either by visible hooks or by concealed fastenings which are operated by drop-handles or knobs. Make sure all are released before endeavouring to raise the lid. The fractured remains of the slim brass hooks which secured their lid flaps against warping can be seen at the right-hand end of countless eighteenth-century square pianos.

When a lid is distorted or warped, considerable strain is thrown on its fastenings. Take up this strain by applying gentle pressure to the top surface of the lid before opening or closing the fastening beneath.

Lock keeps and the eyes engaged by the lid hooks are often let into material of no great thickness and secured by screws whose length affords insufficient purchase to resist mishandling.

Many harpsichords and earlier pianos have separate foreboards to close off the keywell area. If such a foreboard is furnished with a lock, check that the front flap is free before endeavouring to raise it and restrain the foreboard in the process to prevent it falling. Do not leave foreboards lying around where they can be damaged.

Where the lid-prop is a separate item and not hinged to the cheekpiece of the instrument, make sure that it is within reach of one hand before raising the lid with the other. If the ends of the prop are bevelled, make sure the faces are correctly offered to lid and case. Where no special housings are present, support the bottom of the prop in the angle formed by the cheekpiece and the cheekpiece moulding and not on the edge of the soundboard. Make sure that the top of the prop is securely restrained by the lid moulding and that the moulding itself is not loose. In instruments in which the lid is designed to open beyond the vertical, make sure that the cord intended to restrain it remains adequate for the purpose and that it is securely attached.

In opening and closing the lids of harpsichords which incorporate a nag's-head swell, bear in mind the mechanical linkage involved between pedal and swell and avoid forcing it into or out of engagement. Even greater care should be taken in raising or lowering the secondary, louvred lid of instruments with a Venetian swell. Such devices are heavy and awkward to handle. If the swell mechanism is temporarily to be dispensed with, the frame of louvres is most safely raised by one person while another holds open the lid. The secure positioning of the lid-prop is of even greater importance when it supports the combined weight of lid and swell. Assistance is equally desirable in lowering the swell mechanism.

Some instruments have front lid flaps which open back beyond the comfortable reach of someone standing at the keyboard. Handle them from the cheekpiece side, folding back the flap with the left hand and supporting it towards the centre with the right.

In instruments with two hinged front flaps, avoid raising or lowering one flap by the other and throwing unnecessary strain on the hinge screws. Fold back the first flap and move to the cheekpiece of the instrument. Hold the first flap with the right hand and the second with the left. Keep the first lid flap horizontal while folding both back towards the tail of the instrument.

In many square pianos, the two hinged flaps which make up the front section of the lid have bevelled edges where they meet each other at the treble end of the keywell. In closing such a lid, make sure that the right-hand flap is shut before the left.

Lids left constantly open tend to sag. Shut them after use or display and in so doing avoid closing them on to lid props, jack rails, damper rulers and lid closures in their shut position. Some music desks are of deck-chair complexity. Make sure that they are in completely closed order before lowering the lid.

Legs and stands

The legs and stands of most instruments are designed to afford vertical support and not to resist the strains imposed by pulling them along floors or carpets. Earlier instrument stands often comprise a pair of two-legged frames, coach-bolted into two stretchers. Since they are designed to be dismantled when necessary, the tenons of the stretchers are not as snug a fit in their mortices as those which form part of permanent, glued joints. Great care should be taken not to loosen them further.

Where castors are fitted, they should not be employed in the movement of an instrument from one place to another. Many castors were designed with an eye to elegance rather than efficiency and wear has rendered them still less serviceable. Exceptions are some modern grands whose legs are equipped with patent rollers or mounted on steel trolley frames. (Castors can also cause great damage to floors.)

Moving instruments

Some instrument stands are equipped with pedals for the operation of mechanisms within the instrument. Rods and linkages should be disconnected before instrument and stand are parted.

If there are locating battens on the underside of an instrument, their relation with the top rails of the stand should also be observed.

Some linkages are awkward to re-engage. The sostenuto mechanism of those Broadwood squares which have 'peacock' under-dampers is operated by a pull-down which extends well up into the instrument. In this and all other cases of possible difficulty it is a sensible precaution to check that linkages can be reconnected before the relationship between stand and instrument is disturbed.

Without the restraint of their attendant rods, the pedals themselves are free to flap about on their hinges. Whoever moves the stand should avoid catching the pedals on the floor, particularly when the stand is being set down in its new position. It should also be borne in mind that stands are almost as wide as the instruments they support. A number of dents in the architraves of doorways must have been caused by the front ends of harpsichord stands proving obstinately wider than the tail ends.

Professional harpsichord hirers work single-handed wonders with trolleys and instrument shoes but they do not commonly move valuable antiques.

36. A harpsichord by Abraham and Joseph Kirckman at Tatton Park, dated 1789

With one person to move the stand, three others are required to move safely all but the smallest harpsichords, one taking the weight of the tail, each of the others taking one of the front corners. Avoid damage to the side of the instrument from belt buckles; if one person alone is to carry the front of the instrument, the foreboard is particularly vulnerable in this regard.

If more help is available, and for the movement of heavier instruments like all but the earliest pianos it may be essential, five people make up a more efficient team than four, though the negotiation of doorways becomes more difficult. The efforts of a fourth person at the spine or the bentside unbalance the activities of the other three.

If a harpsichord is to be moved up or down stairs, it should be carried the same way round in both cases: tail first in ascent, keyboard first in descent. Bear in mind that though the weight falls more heavily on those carrying the front, the instrument will tend to slip from the grasp of whomever is carrying the tail. The negotiation of stairs too narrow for an instrument to remain flat is more difficult to accomplish safely and therefore not advised unless absolutely unavoidable.

Virginals and spinets can safely be moved by two people, again with a third person being responsible for the stand. Remember that bentside spinets have an odd centre of gravity and that the treble end of the keyboard will require support.

Earlier square pianos are light enough for two to handle, but instruments like the Longman and Broderips of the 1790s are awkward to lift from and replace on their French stands. Some examples have finger reliefs in the top of their back rails, but the location of the piano within the top moulding of the stand remains an awkward operation. The instrument is best aligned in the length, held clear of the stand by the locating dowels if these exist, before being moved forward into position from underneath.

Four people are needed to move the later square pianos. A vast increase in the thickness of their bottom boards and framing, as well as the inclusion of cast-iron members to resist the increased tension of their heavier stringing, makes them prodigiously heavy for their size.

Moving grand pianos, particularly over any great distance, is best left to teams of professionals. Wisdom is not an automatic adjunct of strength, however, and the value and vulnerability of the instrument should be stressed. If the legs are to be removed, care should be taken to ensure that each is reintroduced into its correct housing and that pedal lyres are removed with caution and replaced correctly.

Whenever an instrument is to be moved, one person should be in charge and should make clear to all concerned what is to be involved in the operation. A ruler is a more efficient tool for measuring the width of a doorway than is the instrument itself. The best time for discussion is before an instrument is uplifted, as the removal trade used to have it, rather than after the operation has begun.

In spite of the example afforded by one-man bands, instruments should be carried separately, no matter how small. Flutes, oboes, recorders and the like may have dried-out joints and tend to fall apart. When an instrument has a case, it should be used.

Handstops, pedals, etc.

Many keyboard instruments are furnished with handstops, pedals, knee-levers or other controls, the use of which should be denied to those not conversant with their function, otherwise damage may result.

An obvious example is afforded by the Venetian swell. In the later English harpsichords most commonly equipped with the device, it is usually controlled by a pedal on the right-hand side of the stand. Any endeavour to operate the pedal while the main lid is closed will be not only ineffective but eventually damaging, since movement of the louvres will be impossible and the mechanism subjected to undesirable stress.

A slightly more common feature in English harpsichords is a pedal designed to facilitate changes in registration by achieving in one movement of the foot what would otherwise require the movement of one or more handstops. Such devices are usually operated by a pedal on the left-hand side of the stand. They vary in complexity but appear in their most elaborate form as the machine stop on double manual harpsichords with lute stops.

37. A double manual harpsichord by Shudi & Broadwood, 1770. The louvres of the Venetian swell are shown open

When such a machine is engaged, the force of a spring pulls on the dog-leg and 4-foot registers and pushes off the lute. Pressure on the pedal overcomes the force of the spring, pushing off the dog-leg and 4-foot and bringing on the lute register. The lower manual 8-foot remains hand-controlled. In its on position, it forms part of the full harpsichord chorus when the machine stop is engaged but its pedal not depressed, and affords a lower manual contrast to the lute stop on the upper manual when the machine pedal is operated.

Such machine stops are engaged and disengaged by moving a stop lever which projects through the spine of the instrument at the left-hand side of the keywell. A movement of 10–12mm ($\frac{1}{2}$ in) is involved, towards the tail of the instrument to engage the mechanism, towards the front to disengage it. Slight pressure on the pedal facilitates movement of the knob in both directions.

If an appreciation of the functioning of the mechanism is needed, it can be gained by removing the screws which secure its cover to the outside of the spine. The movements involved will be apparent, as will the considerable strength of the spring necessary to achieve them. The possibility of damage through misuse will be evident.

It should be remembered that the movement of engaging or disengaging the machine stop may leave registers neither fully on nor fully off. Whatever registration is subsequently desired must be set by hand.

The handstops of harpsichords control lateral movements within the instrument and for that reason should be moved sideways, rather than pushed or pulled. Some forward and backward movement of the knobs results from the cranking of the levers they control but this is incidental to their functioning. Some few mid-eighteenth-century Flemish instruments equipped with bell-cranks or inclined planes exist as exceptions to this rule.

The movements involved are small. Some registers move scarcely 1mm between their on and off positions and the movement of their attendant handstops is little more. Even a harp rack moves only about 2mm ($\frac{1}{12}$ in).

A harp rack should not be left engaged when an instrument is not in use, otherwise the pressure of the strings will cause indentations in, or leave rust or oxide deposits on, the buffalo hide or other leather employed in the stop. This applies not only to harpsichords but to those earlier square pianos which have a similar device. In some of these instruments, the lever controlling the harp stop can be mistaken for one of two others which relate to the divided sostenuto mechanism. Normally, the harp stop is controlled by the lever which lies below the other two.

The sostenuto mechanism of such instruments should not be left engaged either. When the piano is not in use, the dampers should be left in contact with the strings, otherwise the whalebone springs which ensure their smart return will be weakened.

As a general rule, when any instrument is not in use, those moving parts which can be relieved of strain should be. This applies not only to things like the pedals of double action harps but to the hair of the bows of instruments of the violin family.

In early grand pianos in which lateral movement of the keyboard can be achieved by the use of a pedal to produce *una corda* effects, a small dovetail wedge is sometimes let into the right-hand keyblock to limit the sideways travel of the action and produce a *due corde* result. In those few examples in which the wedge can be raised above the keyblock, it should not be so left when not in use but pushed back down into the safety of its recess.

Keyboard movement in a front-to-back direction was the means usually chosen on the Continent to couple and uncouple harpsichord manuals. The system was also in use, both here and abroad, to couple the manuals of tracker action organs before tumbler or ram couplers became the norm. In double-manual instruments it is normally, though not always, the upper manual which shifts – away from the player to couple, towards the player to uncouple. In an organ, small spurs were often mounted on the keys of both manuals, and their size and half-round profile render them less liable to damage. In the harpsichord, the system operates by the engagement or otherwise with the upper manual keylevers of wooden dogs mounted on the lower. Their shape and length render them more vulnerable than the organ variety.

The risk of damage is increased by the existence of some modern harpsi-chords with shift couplers which are furnished with spring-loaded dollies instead of rigid dogs. These enable the upper manual to be moved without damage to the mechanism, even though lower manual keys are depressed. A roller system prevents the upper manual jamming even when purchase is applied only to the bass or treble end.

In the classical instrument, it is essential that lower manual keys are not depressed while the upper manual is being moved, otherwise the coupler dogs may be broken off by the distal ends of the upper manual keys. It follows that both hands are free to move the upper manual, each grasping one of the keyblocks to do so.

Cleaning, polishing and dusting

It is to be hoped that smaller instruments of the woodwind group, as well as those of the violin family, will normally be kept in their cases and therefore not require the attention of a cleaner.

If smaller instruments are left on view and require cleaning, bear in mind the vulnerable nature of such things as the tables of lutes, in particular of their roses, and the bellies of violins, especially the areas around the 'f' holes.

Unless their formulation is known and has been approved, avoid pro-prietary cleaners of all sorts, whatever the claims made for them on their labels as 'varnish revivers'. A clean, soft cloth will suffice to remove dust from all areas of such instruments except those too intricate or delicate to tackle. For these, the softest of small brushes and the blowing action of a vacuum cleaner will prove effective.

This blowing and brushing technique should be used to clean harp-lutes, harp-guitars and the other similar instruments designed to fill the space left in the Victorian drawing-room by the removal of the harp proper to the concert hall (for which its growing potential, complexity and cost increasingly suited it).

The moving parts of instruments, like the forks, levers, plates and studs in the actions of post-Hochbrucker harps, are best not touched during routine cleaning, and the same applies to the actions of keyboard instruments. These areas should remain relatively clean and dust is preferable to damage.

Stringed keyboard instruments have their own defences against dusters in the form of hitch- and bridge-pins. If dust builds up for any reason on the soundboard of such an instrument it should be blown out, away from the action, but no endeavour made to remove it in any other way. In the case of a painted soundboard, even blowing dust from the surface should not be attempted if there is any doubt about the stability of the paint.

Brushing the dust from soundboards is not to be recommended. Access is made difficult by the presence of strings, and dirt will tend to accumulate in those areas which are awkward to reach. The roses of English and Italian virginals, of many south European harpsichords and of the earlier guitars, are often vulnerable creations of leather, vellum or fine fretwork. They should not be disturbed by cleaning.

Cleaning should never be carried out on areas of casework which are damaged or unsound. Particularly avoid introducing wax polish into cracks which may subsequently be repaired. Polish renders unfinished surfaces impossible to glue satisfactorily and a split which might have been closed will have to be spliced instead.

Beware of loose veneers. Stringers and inlay, whether of wood or metal, like the Boulle decoration of some nineteenth-century pianos, are particularly liable to lift because of the difference between their rates of contraction and expansion and that of the carcase material beneath.

Never clean fretwork with a duster but use a soft brush and great care. The short-grain features of many of the designs which decorate music desks and nameboards are very easily damaged.

Never use metal polishes on brass or silver instruments or on the metal furniture of others. Apart from creating an undesirably new look by removing the patination, the abrasive effect of such polishes destroys the crispness of the original design, rubs out the repoussé work which decorates, for example, the lid hinges of many earlier English bentside spinets, removes gold from items that may look like brass but are in fact ormolu or brass-gilt, and leaves a stubbornly persistent deposit around the feature cleaned.

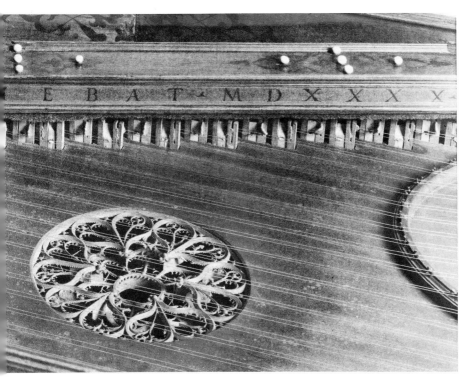

38. A polygonal virginal by Marcus Siculus, 1540; detail showing the rose and jackrail

Take extreme care in removing dust from painted, gilded or papered surfaces. Such finishes can only be as stable as the material they decorate and the adhesives used in their application. Movement in the one and failure in the other can lead to flaking and peeling.

ENEMIES AND SNAGS

The atmosphere

The effects of high humidity on wood, leather, felt and other hygroscopic materials can be imagined: expansion due to water absorption, distortion and consequent malfunction. The formation of mould growths is encouraged. The strength of water-reversible adhesives is reduced.

High humidity also encourages the formation of deposits on metal items such as the fulcra on which moving parts turn. In extreme cases, iron balance pins can not only rust solidly into the mortices of the early keyboards in which they are encountered but can actually destroy the material of the surrounding keylevers. Rusty tuning pins can similarly affect a wrestplank.

39. The Music Room at Snowshill Manor

Humid conditions can rapidly lead to the formation of sufficient oxide on key-loadings to jam adjacent keys, especially when the same conditions provoke distortion of the levers themselves. The gold leaf applied to the lead roses of many north European harpsichords can be dulled and eventually penetrated if oxide is able to form underneath.

Conditions of low humidity result in the loss of cellular moisture in wooden parts, leading to distortion and splitting. Oddly, some baizes and felts tend initially to expand and become fluffier as they dry out. Leather shrinks and eventually perishes altogether. In dry conditions, organ pallets cease to be wind-tight and leaks appear in bellows and trunking. The use of electric blowers to supply instruments previously hand-pumped can accentuate the problem since the air may be warmed in its passage through the blower and its relative humidity reduced.

The range of relative humidity within which musical instruments are best conserved is 50–60 per cent, bearing in mind the slightly conflicting demands of their component parts. In endeavouring to preserve the ideal of 55 per cent, avoid sudden changes, since these are more damaging than gradual alterations. The introduction of efficient heating systems into churches previously without them brings work to the organ builders when it might perhaps better bring work to the humidification experts. The same problem is encountered in a house with the advent of each new heating season and particular care should be taken at that time of year. The situation is aggravated by the fact that the humidity of cold winter air is normally much lower than that of warm summer air and an increase of perhaps 16 centigrade (30 Fahrenheit) degrees in the temperature of dry winter air indoors can produce a most dangerous drop in the relative humidity.

Alterations in temperature are rather less serious *per se* but obviously affect the relative humidity and, again, sudden changes should be avoided. The most obvious effect is on the tuning of instruments. Considerable heat is generated by the additional lighting involved in film and television work. Remember this when there are camera crews in the house.

Instruments are not usually subjected to conditions of extreme cold. If they are, however, a phenomenon known as allotropy can occur, in which metal parts such as the lead-gilt roses of harpsichords and the tin alloy pipes of organs can actually crumble into powder.

The regular inspection of instruments is essential, of those kept in their cases or in store as well as those on display. Poorly ventilated surroundings encourage mould growth, particularly when the atmosphere is hot and humid.

Of the airborne pollutants, the chlorides are the most corrosive of metal items but their presence in quantity is only likely in industrial or marine environments. Of the harmful airborne gases, sulphur dioxide is particularly destructive of leather, felt and baize. It is more likely to be a problem in urban environments. If either of these is causing damage, instruments must be kept covered by glass or dust-sheets when not in use or on display.

Pests

Woodworm and moth are the two parasites most likely to attack musical instruments. A constant watch must be kept for evidence of the activity of either pest.

Woodworm have dietary preferences and are particularly likely to relish the pine and spruce-fir of which most soundboards are made, the beech commonly used for bridges and nuts and the walnut casework of English bentside spinets. Many other woods are liable to attack, however, though worm activity in some timbers like oak tends to be concentrated in the sapwood rather than in the heart. Animal glues also attract woodworm, and damage often runs along the line of a joint.

Left unchecked, woodworm can irreversibly damage an instrument. The structural weakness resulting from extensive galleries of activity can often be remedied but tonal alteration is almost bound to result from any of the expedients used to stabilize a severely damaged soundboard, even when the actual replacement of deceased timber is avoided.

Small heaps or tracks of wood dust are commonly looked for as evidence of infestation but such telltales can well remain unobserved within an instrument. The presence of worm is often more certainly diagnosed by looking for fresh flight-holes. These usually appear during April and May, as the grubs which have spent the last one or more years eating their way to maturity emerge and take wing to find suitable locations for the laying of more eggs. Once hatched, these in their turn burrow into the wood to continue the destructive cycle.

Fresh flight-holes can best be seen in a raking light which will reveal the paler colour and sharper arris of recent damage (see Woodworm, p. 90).

The topical application of an insecticide like Cuprinol is not always to be recommended with musical instruments. It can reduce the elasticity and increase the density of the resonating parts of an instrument, with resulting tonal loss. Advice should be sought as to whether a more effective treatment would be the subjection of the instrument to exposure for forty-eight hours to an atmosphere of methyl bromide. Other fumigants can be effective but all of them involve poisonous gas, and treatment must be carried out by specialists.

The wool and other natural fibres which make up the baizes and felts found in many musical instruments are the favourite diet of the larvae of moths. Unfortunately, although the eggs from which the larvae develop can be removed by a vacuum cleaner, they are seldom laid in the most accessible places. A specialized preventive insecticide affords an alternative treatment. Products containing pentachlorophenol can be employed, but should not be used without advice, since the application of any liquid to a material can alter its mechanical properties. Paradichlorobenzene crystals are much more convenient but less effective except in a confined space. The protection which they afford an instrument on display is therefore limited.

Tension and Distortion

Stringed instruments should be kept at or below the pitch for which they were designed. If there is any reason to believe that an instrument is unable to withstand this tension, or any ground for thinking that the string gauges have been increased during earlier repairs, the load should be reduced evenly throughout the compass. The pitch of the instrument should be lowered by a third or fourth and advice sought about the structural instability which provoked the anxiety.

The effects of distortion are difficult to remedy in the workshop. Modern restoration practice properly rejects the use of reinforcement and the alternative, if it must be undertaken, can involve the complete disassembly of an instrument.

In guitars and lutes, distortion is commonly seen in the deepening of the action as the neck pulls forward. The longer the neck, the more acute the possible problem; chitarrones (large long-necked lutes) are particularly vulnerable. Tension can also distort the tables of instruments whose strings are hitched to the bridge, rather than being secured to a tail-piece or tail-buttons. The more lightly barred the belly, the more susceptible the instrument; the earlier guitar is therefore much at risk.

The effect of tension on the various stringed keyboard instruments is obviously directly related to the ability of their framing to withstand the load imposed. Increases in the compass and sustaining power of the piano, for example, were not always matched by adequate increases in structural strength. If proper consideration is given to their original string gauges and probable pitch, however, wooden-framed instruments are not necessarily unstable; nor are later pianos, particularly those examples with metal spreaders and hitchplates rather than complete cast frames, necessarily stable.

String tension is responsible for the distortion of numbers of square pianos. The cases of the earlier examples tend to lift from the horizontal at the front-right-hand or back-left-hand corner. The foreboards of such instruments become jammed when shut and removal of their nameboards for action regulation is difficult because they are pinched between the returns of the keywell.

The framing typical of the eighteenth-century harpsichord made in this country seems to have contributed to the dropping of the cheekpiece at its junction with the bentside, a distortion so frequently encountered that it is commonly called 'the English accent'. The top edge of the bentside is frequently pulled in and the junction between bentside and tail is often distorted. Action gaps between wrestplank and belly-rail tend to close and hitchpin rails to pull away from the case sides. Four-foot bridges are often pushed downwards and 4-foot hitchpin rails often pulled up. Wrestplanks can bend both forwards and upwards, become insecurely anchored and in some cases split their housings in spine or cheekpiece. Italian instruments, especially those lightly constructed virginals and harpsichords with separate outer cases, can literally curl up under tension.

The bows of instruments of the violin and viol family can suffer in the

same way. Pernambuco and snakewood sticks lose their elegant and functional shape unless relieved of the tension of the horsehair after use.

Instruments should be inspected at least once a year for signs of such
distortion. Remember that if an instrument is not tuned regularly, conditions
can combine to produce a rise rather than a fall in pitch and a resulting
increase in the tension. The load on a harpsichord with three choirs of
strings, for instance, increases by more than a quarter of a ton if its pitch is
raised by a semitone. For this reason, advice must be sought before an
instrument designed for a lower pitch is tuned to a higher, a request most
likely to be made by those who wish to use it in concert with a modern flute
or oboe, for example.

Tuners

Present-day piano-tuners are not infrequently skilled technicians, capable
also of carrying out not only the regulation but the mechanical repair of the
modern instruments which they commonly encounter. The same is true of
organ-tuners, for whom tuning is likely to be only a part of the skilled work
they do for the firms who employ them. Neither, though, may be sympathetic
to or conversant with historical examples of the instruments with which they
deal.

Care must therefore be taken in the choice of tuners. Open metal pipework
is not best attended to by those accustomed only to tuning slides; slim,
oblong-headed wrestpins must be protected from ill-fitting tuning hammers
in the hands of those who instinctively 'set' the pins.

Recommendations offered about regulation and repair should be treated
with caution, and advice obtained before they are implemented. Proposals
involving any degree of modification or 'improvement' should be rejected.
The authentic pitch, or an approved alternative, should be preserved, as
should the tuning of those instruments for which the temperament can be
deduced.

Conservators

The number of instrument-makers devoting their attention to building copies
of historical originals has vastly increased over the last twenty years. Skills
and scholarship vary widely, in the same way that the instruments available
range from assembled kits to valuable examples of the work of excellent and
informed craftsmen.

It is important to remember that even a good instrument-maker is not
necessarily a good conservator. The techniques, disciplines and attitudes
involved are subtly different, and a historical humility is required of the
conservator which is not necessarily demanded of the builder.

A simultaneous though smaller growth can be seen in the numbers of those who specialize in instrument restoration and a similar variation can be seen in scholarship and skill. Proper documentation, in the form of reports, work schedules, photographic records and drawings, is an essential part of the process still too often regarded as an unnecessary chore.

Restoration may not be in all cases the best way of conserving a musical instrument. Improvements in remedial techniques continue to be made. In some instances it may be wiser to do no more than stabilize the condition of an instrument in the hope that repair can be undertaken in the future. A further, perhaps more ethical, consideration is that the use invited by an instrument in playing condition should not be allowed to accelerate its decline.

Advice must be obtained whenever the restoration of an instrument is contemplated.

Specialists and amateurs

The change in musical taste which was initially engendered by but now also sustains the giving of more historically accurate performances of music from the Renaissance to the early Classical period has been attended by growing interest in textual accuracy, in performing practice and, obviously, in the instruments themselves. Requests from both specialists and amateurs to examine, measure and play instruments of historical interest are increasingly frequently received by those who own them.

Such interest is to be encouraged, but the well-being of the instruments must remain of paramount importance. Damage can be caused by the enthusiastic but uninformed researcher, especially if any degree of disassembly is involved in the taking of measurements or the making of drawings.

The playing of instruments not in a condition to be played is to be discouraged, since mechanical damage can result. Even the blowing of experimental passages on woodwind or brass instruments causes internal condensation which, if not disposed of, may damage the instrument. Serpents have suffered seriously in this way.

The matter of alterations in pitch for performance purposes has been mentioned. In this and in all cases in which requests are received to play or make detailed examinations of instruments, expert advice should be sought.

✻

For musical boxes, see p. 234.

The roseate hues of early dawn,
The brightness of the day,
The crimson of the sunset sky,
How fast they fade away.

Mrs C. F. Alexander, from
Hymns Ancient and Modern,
1861 edition

PHOTOGRAPHS

40. William Henry Fox Talbot, one of the pioneers of modern photography, from a
daguerrotype of about 1850 at Lacock Abbey

·✣ PHOTOGRAPHS ✣·

It is only in recent years that the historic value of photography has come to be realized. Unique examples must exist in many English houses, and there may well be members of the family or people living locally who can identify the subjects of old photographs.

BLACK-AND-WHITE PHOTOGRAPHS AND PHOTOGRAPH ALBUMS

A photograph is essentially a chemically sensitized paper which has reacted to exposure to light and produced an image after chemical processing. The image layer is frequently unstable and particularly sensitive to deterioration by light and pollution. The paper layer is subject to the same problems as all paper items, but especially to fluctuations in relative humidity.

Cartes-de-visite, card mounts, coloured backboards in frames and card-album pages were made from poor-quality ground wood pulp, and so are highly acidic and discolour and deteriorate rapidly. Thus, although the paper layer itself may be of good quality, migration of acidic by-products from supports and their manner of attachment will cause deterioration.

Storage and display

Relative humidity and temperature should be kept as constant as possible, as variations will cause expansion and contraction of the photographic emulsions and lead to cracking and flaking. Temperature should not exceed 15°C (60°F) and relative humidity should be between 45 and 55 per cent. Mould growth will be encouraged in a relative humidity of over 60 per cent and there is unfortunately no recommended fungicide for photographs.

Photographs should be stored in the dark. On display, light should be restricted to 50 lux maximum with an ultraviolet filter. Tungsten lights may need heat filters.

Never touch the surface of the image. Collections that are handled, for study purposes, for example, should be stored in transparent polyester envelopes with acid-free card supports for fragile or large items. Any adhesive seam should be positioned on the reverse side of the image. Sellotape should be avoided.

Never store photographs near or in wood furniture, or in newly painted or varnished areas. Wood gives off peroxides which react adversely with the image layer. Ideal storage would be an enamel-finish steel cabinet with air vents, fitted with dust filters, in a clean, dry area. Mounted photographs can be stored in acid-free boxes and kept on open shelves. Albums should be wrapped in strong acid-free paper and tied with flat cloth tape until they can be boxed.

Atmospheric pollutants which degrade photographs include:

(a) ozone, given off, for example, by photocopying machines
(b) hydrogen sulphide, nitrogen, oxides in the air
(c) peroxides, given off by wood, bleaches
(d) ammonia from household cleaners
(e) sulphur from deteriorating rubber, e.g. rubber adhesives such as Evo-stik, etc., rubber bands, etc.
(f) salt carried by coastal winds; this is hygroscopic and therefore relative humidity must be monitored carefully.

Photographic copies can be made through the polyester envelopes recommended. Commissions for new photographs and orders for copies should include the necessary processing recommendations for maximum permanence. (Consult a paper conservator.) For instance, a mirror-like surface which develops on the darker areas of photographs indicates that excess sodium thiosulphate has been deposited during processing. Resin-coated photographic papers are not recommended for archival use; photographs should not be dry mounted. Acid-free card mounts should be specified.

Specific problems

Gelatine photographs

These are especially subject to cracking and flaking – usually caused by high relative humidity – and mould and insect attack, such as silverfish.

Nitrate film

This was in use from 1899 to 1939, and is a severe fire risk, as chemical decomposition can produce spontaneous combustion. Film should be copied and the original destroyed or stored at a temperature between 2 and 5°C (36 and 41°F). Cellulose acetate film only became generally available about 1930.

Daguerrotypes, Ambrotypes

Never touch the surface. Store in the original cases wherever possible and keep closed. Do not attempt to clean the surround – a velvet or gilt frame, for example – as the dislodged dust particles will damage the image surface.

Lantern slides and glass negatives

These should be isolated from each other by the recommended transparent polyester envelopes (see Appendix 4, p. 256), and stored in their original boxes in cupboards. Do not attempt to stick broken photographs together (glass or paper). Keep all relevant pieces in a labelled envelope until the problem can be discussed with a conservator.

41. A screen with Victorian family photographs in the library at Clandon

COLOUR PHOTOGRAPHS

These were commercially in use and widely available by the 1950s, although early colour processes, such as Autochrome, were selectively available from the late 1930s.

Colour photographs are subject to the same problems as black-and-whites, but especially to fluctuations of relative humidity, and to fading. The rate of fading is thought to be related to the film speed, lower film speeds giving a more permanent colour image.

In order to maximize the permanence of these images, exposure of original photographs should be avoided. Duplicates should be used for study and exhibition.

Storage

Ideally the temperature should be between 2 and 5°C (36 and 41°F), but a constant temperature between 8 and 12° (46 and 54°F) is acceptable, with the relative humidity constant between 30 and 45 per cent. Otherwise store as for black-and-white photographs.

The way to ensure summer in England is to have it framed and glazed in a comfortable room.

Horace Walpole,
letter to Dr William Cole, 28 May 1774

When Sir Joshua Reynolds died
All Nature was degraded;
The King dropped a tear into the Queen's ear
And all his pictures faded.

William Blake, *On Art and Artists*

42 and 43. Nash's original design for the Picture Gallery at Attingham and (below) as it is today

·✤ PAINTINGS ✤·

Pictures play an essential role in the embellishment of any country house and many country-house collections contain paintings and frames of outstanding importance. The continued enjoyment of a picture depends on its survival in good condition.

The surface of a painting should not be touched by anyone but a picture conservator. In fact once a picture is hanging safely on the wall, it is best left entirely alone; even dusting the frame exposes the painting to risks of accidental damage.

The care of pictures through good housekeeping falls into three areas: avoidance of accidental damage; observing and reporting suspected deterioration; and maintaining an appropriate and stable environment.

PREVENTING ACCIDENTAL DAMAGE

Much of the repair work of paintings is made necessary by accidental damage received in the course of handling, storage and display. All possible steps should therefore be taken to minimize risks.

Visitors and house staff

Pictures should wherever possible be safeguarded by placing furniture below them. Topographical views in particular tempt visitors to point out local features. Room stewards should discourage visitors from pointing at details in paintings as the distance may be misjudged or the hand accidentally jolted. Apart from the risk of inadvertent damage, fingers deposit grease and grime on the painted surface.

Paintings should not be hung where they are liable to be knocked by visitors pushing through narrow passages or bottlenecks; nor in vulnerable positions on staircases. Any painting that is in danger of being knocked or scraped and which cannot be hung elsewhere should be glazed.

Be aware of the vulnerability of pictures when moving furniture and other objects in a room. Always have at least two people to carry long objects such as ladders, especially on staircases where paintings suffer from window-cleaners' ladders. Never allow one person to move tall step-ladders single-handed, as they are easily unbalanced.

Tower scaffolding should be erected and dismantled well away from the paintings; avoid loose tools on the platform which could drop down on to a painting.

Never hold a tool above a picture or attempt to position something above a painting. First remove the painting right out of the way. This also applies when taking down or hanging one painting above another. Always take down the lower register before handling the upper register.

While in principle no work should take place above a painting, in some circumstances it is impractical to take down all the pictures before dusting cornices with a vacuum cleaner. In this case it is often wiser to leave a little dust than to endanger a painting.

When planned ahead, it is generally possible to arrange for a picture conservator to be working in the house while special cleaning, which gives rise to these problems, is taking place.

Try to avoid creating dust in a room, especially when dry-sweeping a stone floor. Avoid leaving excessive damp after washing a floor, because this could combine with chemical deposits from industrial pollution and cause a bloom to form on the surface of varnished paintings.

Aerosols and other sprays must not be allowed in the vicinity of pictures. Do not use insecticides or oil-based pesticides, such as Cuprinol or Rentokil, on picture frames or any part of the paintings, such as panels or stretcher bars, as the non-volatile base can cause serious damage.

Building and decorating

Always remove paintings out of the way of builders and their scaffolding. Paintings should not be left in an area where decorations or repairs are to be carried out.

Never hang a painting on a freshly plastered wall until the wall has quite dried out, which may be a matter of months; nor in a newly painted room until the smell has dispersed. Smell is an indication of chemical change. Emulsion and oil-based paints undergo chemical modification during drying.

The redecoration of a room presents a good opportunity to remove and treat paintings in fixed architectural frames. Also where special scaffolding is needed, such as on staircases, the conservation of the paintings can be planned ahead to coincide with building work.

Paintings set in panelling or fixed architectural frames had space allowed for air movement and were not set directly on to brick or rendered walls. Never plaster or paint behind a painting set in the wall. Modern plastic paints should not be used on the wall surrounding a painting inset into the wall, or round a wall-painting, because any dampness in the wall could then only come out behind the painting or through the wall-painting.

Photography and filming

See that all equipment is kept well clear of paintings and other objects, to avoid accidental damage. The desire to help the media, or earn money from publicity, must take second place to the prime duty of protecting the objects.

For example, chandeliers have been damaged by photographers moving their equipment round a room without proper supervision.

Oil paintings on canvas are less vulnerable to exposure to tungsten halogen lights (as used in photo-floods) than are textiles, drawings and water-colours. However, even short periods of floodlighting can raise the temperature and lower the relative humidity.

Photo-flood lights should always be kept at least 1.5 m (5 ft) away from all picture surfaces. There should be adequate ventilation such as open windows, cooling fans and reflectors, to deflect the heat, and the lights must be switched off immediately after the photograph has been taken.

When photographing pictures, photographers should not be left alone with the painting and no picture should be handled or unframed by the photographer. A glazed water-colour, print, drawing, etc., must never be unframed except by experts. Sealing works of art on paper into a frame is a specialized job which only a few framers do correctly.

44. This illustrates the eighteenth-century practice of hanging pictures from chair rail to cornice at Saltram

Photographers should not be allowed to touch the surface of the painting in any way, and should on no account be allowed to wipe the surface, either dry or with any liquid.

ACTION IN THE EVENT OF DAMAGE

In the case of a painting being damaged, advice should be sought without delay from a picture conservator.

Accidents

If damage such as a dent, scrape or tear is found, do not take the painting down, and avoid the almost irresistible temptation to touch the surface. Give details of the nature, location and extent of the damage to a picture conservator.

If the painting has fallen off the wall or has been badly jolted, record the incident, even if there is no apparent damage, so that the picture and frame can be checked carefully on the next visit of a picture conservator. Before moving the painting, check whether any chips of paint have fallen off newly damaged areas in case these could be retrieved from the frame, furniture or floor by the picture conservator. Do not touch the damaged surface of the painting.

Floods, splashes

If the picture has been splashed with a liquid or streaked by water from a burst pipe, do not wipe the surface. Leave the painting hanging unless it is necessary to remove it from further risk. Do not be alarmed if the varnish becomes opaque and white as it dries.

If the painting has been in a flood, take it down and lay it flat, *face upwards*, supporting its frame on blocks so that the air can circulate underneath. Be sure that the blocks do not touch the back of the painting. It should be left to dry out in a well-ventilated room with no extra heating and in a safe place where no one will step on it.

Birds' mess

If birds habitually fly into a room, stretch soft fruit cage netting over the window opening. At a distance, it will be hardly visible.

If a bird gets in by accident, no attempt should be made to remove the white splashes it may leave on the surface of the painting, as there is a danger of rubbing the mess in or smearing it over the surface. The picture conservator should be able to remove it without disturbing the varnish.

CARRYING PICTURES

Before attempting to move a picture, be sure that there are enough helpers and time to do so safely. Most pictures should be carried by two people. One person should be responsible for the front of the painting and the other for the back throughout the operation, so that it can safely be manoeuvred round corners and past door knobs. Decide exactly where you intend moving the painting and inspect the route for hazards. Always carry a painting vertically by its shortest sides. This lowers its centre of gravity and makes it more stable and manageable. In carrying large paintings particular attention should be given to heights of doors and stair-flights.

Never take hold of a framed painting by anything but the frame. It is very tempting to lift a framed picture by the stretcher bars of the painting, but the canvas would then be taking the weight of the frame and painting. Inexperienced furniture removers have to be carefully instructed and supervised.

When carrying unframed paintings fingers should not come into contact with the painted surface.

HANGING AND TAKING DOWN PICTURES

How and where a picture is hung has a great bearing on its preservation. Pictures should not be hung above radiators or on sections of wall carrying hot pipes or internal flues which can heat up the wall quite considerably. Hanging pictures above a fireplace which is in use cannot be recommended. In no case should a fire be lit under panel paintings. If the dining-room is used, hot plates or greasy, steaming dishes should not be placed below a painting. (See also Environment, p. 156.)

Air should circulate to the back of a picture – normally the frame leans forwards at a slight angle so that only the bottom edge touches the wall. Outside walls are subject to condensation so stick corks to the bottom corners of the frame to isolate the picture from the wall completely and to allow maximum circulation of air.

In most houses there is a traditional method of hanging which should be followed. In a room without picture rails and where picture chains or wires do not need to be visible, hang the painting from two screws plugged into the wall. Fix two hooks on the back of the frame and suspend it on short lengths of picture chain. The positioning of the hooks on the side members will control the forward tilt of the painting.

Check periodically that the fixings and fittings on walls and frames are sound and that chains, wires or cords are in good condition. Note any that need to be replaced. Wires and cords fray and rot at the fixings.

Large, heavy frames should be supported underneath to prevent the mitres from opening under the strain. Upper-register paintings can be canted forward by being supported at the base and by lowering the hooks on the frame

45 and 46. Different methods of picture hanging: (above) with cords in the Stone Hall at Uppark; (right) an unusual hanging of enamels on brass rails in the drawing-room at Kingston Lacy

towards the centre of the side members. In every case where the weight of the frame is resting on a support, a short length of picture wire should be twisted through the link of the picture chain to prevent the hook from disengaging.

When hanging a painting, check that there are no obstructions in contact with the back of the painting such as alarm systems, picture-light wires or plugs. When picture wire is used, check that no loose ends are touching the back of the canvas which could later cause a protrusion in the front of the picture.

Before taking down a painting, remove all ornaments below the picture as well as any furniture that would get in the way. If the painting is hung on a picture chain, slip a treasurer's filing tag or a paperclip into the link of both chains from which the picture is hanging. This saves all the time and bother of re-establishing the correct height and level when rehanging the painting.

When lifting the picture clear of the wall, make sure that nothing can fall down and hit the front or back of the picture. This is particularly important where there is a heavy hook over a picture rail. A bang on the back of the canvas will cause whorled craquelure on the painted surface and the damage is irreparable. Keep the painting vertical when lowering it gently to the floor. A plain carved frame should be tipped slightly backwards so that it rests on the straight edge behind the carved moulding.

If the picture is in a decorated carved frame or in a fragile plaster frame, lower it on to a padded surface made up of, say, two bolsters placed on the floor at right angles to the wall; or use offcuts of rubber-backed carpet, which a local carpet dealer should be able to supply free, and which have the additional advantage of not slipping.

STORING: LONG-TERM AND TEMPORARY

Conditions

Suitable long-term storage room in a house open to visitors should be planned at the same time as space is allocated for shops, tearooms and information centres.

Do not store paintings or anything else near boilers, water pipes or in damp areas. Avoid stone floors, which can get cold and damp, and never use a newly painted or plastered room for storage until it has completely dried out and the smell evaporated.

Basements are generally cold and damp or, when the boiler is sited there, hot and damp. Attics should be used only if the roof is insulated, because otherwise the temperature can drop below freezing in winter or heat up unacceptably in summer.

The greatest care should be taken over the conditions in a store-room because the objects in store are inspected less often than when displayed in a room. The relative humidity should be checked at regular intervals and light should be eliminated by keeping shutters closed or by draping black cloth over the windows. This also helps to control fluctuations in temperature. Draughts should be avoided but ventilation is important.

Methods of storing paintings

Framed pictures are safest hung, so whenever possible hang them like postage stamps on the store-room walls. Avoid external walls. Stick corks on the bottom corners of the back of the frame so that the picture is isolated from any condensation that may form on the wall. Check all fixings, wires and chains so that there is no danger of the picture falling off the wall.

Simple wooden racks can be built if there are more paintings than can be hung on the available wall-space in the store-room.

Temporary stacking

Avoid stacking immediately under windows, near radiators or on a stone floor.

Never put framed and unframed paintings in the same stack.

Ensure that nothing touches the canvas of the painting from the front or the back.

Cover the stack loosely with a lightweight dust-sheet, ensuring that it does not come in contact with the paint surface. A polythene sheet can be placed over the dust-sheet for extra short-term protection particularly if builders are in the house, but it should not prevent air circulation.

Stacking framed paintings

Remove all projections such as picture lights, brackets, wires, chain, etc. If frame hooks are not removed, care must be taken that they do not touch the gilded surface of another frame.

Stack in descending order of size and not more than three deep because the angle of the frame gets progressively less upright and the weight of the stack would rest too heavily on the first picture. Should it be necessary, through lack of space, temporarily to stack more than three deep, place a sheet of hardboard behind the third frame and then stack another two or three frames against the hardboard sheet.

Pads of tissue paper between the frames will protect the gilding from damage during stacking. However in subsequent handling the pads invariably fall down and touch the picture surface.

Paintings in plain frames can be stacked with the painting facing inwards, so that dust will not collect on the painted surface and the stretcher bars give the picture some protection against accidental damage.

Paintings in elaborately carved and decorated frames should not be stacked. Pad the floor with bolsters or equivalent, and lean the frame against the wall face outwards. If necessary a piece of hardboard should be placed against the frame before covering with a dust-sheet.

Stacking unframed paintings

Check that the wall is clear of projections, such as light switches or mouldings. Stack face inwards in order of diminishing size and ensure that only the edge of the picture surface, that would normally rest under the rabbet of the frame, is touching the stretcher bar of the back of the painting against which it is stacked. Paintings in one stack should be more or less of the same size or there is a danger that the corner of the smaller painting will swivel and touch the back of the canvas of the picture in front of it.

FRAMES AND FRAMING

The framing of a painting plays an important role in preserving the painting. Apart from its aesthetic function, a frame protects the edges of the painting and makes handling and storage safer. The same care is needed in selecting frame-makers with a historical knowledge of frames and an understanding of conservation, as is taken in other fields of conservation.

Until the importance and condition of a frame have been established it is advisable not to touch it. Original frames of great importance are too often ruined by modern frame-makers and amateurs alike treating the gilding inappropriately.

Dusting frames

Dusting the picture frame puts the painting at risk. Most country-house picture frames are grimy and cannot be safely cleaned except by a gilder trained in conservation. Dusting the frame will not greatly improve its appearance and it is often better to put up with a little dust rather than put the painting at risk. A picture hanging on the wall is best left entirely alone.

Do not attempt to dust a frame if the gilding is flaking; report any sign of woodworm to a conservator. (No part of a painting or frame should be treated for woodworm by the house staff because the non-volatile base of pesticides could cause serious damage.) A 'bit box' should be kept for any pieces of carving, plaster or other bits that may become detached. Identify the bit and give it to a furniture conservator to refix.

Do not dust with a cloth or feather duster, either of which would abrade the surface. No liquid whatsoever should touch the surface of the frame. A damp cloth would remove water gilding and in the past many frames have been damaged in this way.

If it is decided that a frame can be safely dusted, this is best done when the picture is down off the wall by standing at the back of the frame and dusting the top back edge with a Hoover Dustette. The bottom member of the front of the frame can also be brushed gently with a ponyhair fitch, collecting the dust in a Hoover Dustette.

The surface of the painting should not be touched while dusting the frame and if there is any danger of dust flying on to the painting, it is better to leave the dust settled on the frame.

(Cleaning of glass, see Cleaning frames, pp. 171-2.)

Numbering picture frames

Country-house collections were often numbered and identified on the frame. In houses where this has not been the practice in the past, other ways of giving information to visitors should be considered. One possibility is to have a 'bat' in each room on which is sketched the layout of each wall, with the pictures listed underneath. This is particularly appropriate where ropes keep visitors from approaching the pictures to read the numbers. Where this is not the case, tablets can be hung under the pictures, suspended on chains from the back of the frame. A good example of this method can be seen at Ickworth; it avoids all danger of damaging the carved and gilded face of the frame.

Framing and unframing

It will not normally be necessary for paintings to be framed and unframed in the house, except when conservation is to take place *in situ*.

The picture conservator will provide the brass framing plates and balsa wood spacing pieces and will demonstrate the best methods.

Panels and paintings on metal or unusual materials, such as slate, are delicate and should only be framed and unframed by a picture conservator because there are too many problems that may arise.

Fitting backing boards to framed paintings

A backing board not only protects a painting from accidental damage but reduces the exposure of the canvas to oxidants and pollutants in the atmosphere and so slows the rate of deterioration. The most appropriate way of backing the frames of country-house collections is under review.

TRANSPORT

Any painting that is going to be transported should be carefully inspected to make sure it is not flaking (see Routine inspection, below). If there is flaking the picture must be prepared for transport by a picture conservator.

Only small paintings can be carried safely in a car by an unqualified person. Few trade carriers are experts at transporting paintings. Quite apart from causing damage to a painting, the cost of conservation is very high and good conservators object strongly to spending time repairing avoidable damage through careless handling. The extra cost of specialist picture transporters is worth-while. Never let a painting leave the house unless the driver is accompanied. Otherwise, in case of breakdown, the van would be left unattended.

The painting should be loaded upright, supported on soft padding, covered with clean dust-sheeting and strapped to the van's sides by means of flat webbing.

Unless the painting has been crated, it should not be allowed to travel in a mixed load. Crated pictures must also travel upright and be similarly secured.

See that paintings, whether crated or not, are handled gently and not bumped around. Uncrated paintings should be handled by the frames only and not by the back of the picture stretchers. Only unframed paintings should be handled by the stretcher bars.

ROUTINE INSPECTION

Signs of suspected deterioration can be determined without touching the surface of the picture. Only a picture conservator should touch the surface of a painting.

Flaking

It takes a trained eye to distinguish signs of incipient flaking from natural ageing and the normal craquelure found on all old paintings, but chips of paint that have almost become detached can be noticed easily by standing at the side of the painting and using a torch to provide a raking light on the surface.

Panels

Movement in panel paintings renders them particularly susceptible to flaking.

Look out for independent movement of the members which make up a panel. Old splits have usually been restored and are dark, with old discoloured retouches and grime in the crack. A fresh break would appear light.

Some convex warping is to be expected but watch for signs of change in the curvature. This can be seen by an increase in the gap on the inner sides of the frame between the paint surface and frame rabbet.

In cases of extreme humidity the curve can become concave, which is highly dangerous as the paint surface is then contracted. Notify a conservator immediately if a concave warp is noticed, but do not remove the panel from the room in which it hangs as the change in environment must be most carefully controlled by the picture conservator to avoid cracking and loss of paint.

Canvases

The tension of the canvas may vary with changes in the weather and relative humidity, but this should cause no undue concern. Correct stretching should be left to the picture conservator. However, buckling at corners and edges should be noted and reported.

Occasionally a wedge from the stretcher will slip between the canvas and the bottom stretcher bar and will cause a distortion; accumulations of dust and other matter can have the same effect. *Never* attempt to remove these foreign bodies; leave it to the picture conservator. The reasons for this are that the edges of the canvas of an unlined painting can be weak and can tear away from the stretcher bar. Also foreign matter is easy to shift but difficult to remove. Shifting the obstruction without removing it would distort and bruise the canvas in more than one place, so that twice the amount of damage would be caused.

ENVIRONMENT

One of the difficulties in caring for the contents of a historic house is that the damage caused by negligence is often not immediately apparent. The life of

47. Seventeenth-century portraits in the ballroom at Knole, with Edwardian brass picture lights

a painting will be greatly prolonged by the attention given to maintaining a stable environment.

The supports of most paintings are canvas, wood or copper. All are sensitive to changes of humidity or temperature. Excessive expansion and contraction of the support can lead to lifting and flaking of the paint, which is too rigid to follow these movements.

Stable conditions are easier to maintain in rooms which are panelled or contain textiles, such as wall-hangings, curtains and upholstered furniture, which insulate and absorb moisture, so reducing the danger of sudden changes of temperature and relative humidity.

Slow seasonal changes can be tolerated relatively safely, but if a room has to be heated for a winter function, it should be done gradually to avoid potentially destructive sudden change.

Paintings on wooden panels are particularly susceptible to adverse environmental conditions. Rooms in which important panel paintings hang should have the relative humidity checked regularly and extra readings taken in exceptional circumstances, such as extreme changes in the weather conditions or the heating up of a house for a function. The relative humidity should not fall below 45 per cent.

Daylight

Never let direct sunlight fall on a painting. The cumulative effect of sunlight will greatly accelerate the decay of the painting, although this happens so slowly that it may not be apparent even over a lifetime. As well as heat, ultraviolet rays present in daylight degrade the materials of a painting.

Light falling on the painted surface should not exceed 200 lux. Use the blinds and keep shutters closed whenever possible, to reduce the length of time the picture is exposed to light.

Picture lights

The types of picture light at present available are not recommended from a conservation point of view. They can cause patches of overheating of the picture surface.

Also, existing picture lights do not illuminate the whole surface evenly but reflect pools of light in the varnish. It is sometimes possible to cant forward the upper register of paintings in a room, which reduces reflection and makes it easier for the pictures to be seen without resorting to picture lights.

Never fit picture lights to paintings on wood, metal, paper or vellum. Avoid placing a standard or table lamp immediately beneath a picture because light is also a source of heat. A safer and better way of lighting pictures is currently being developed.

·✤   MINIATURES   ✤·

The term miniature is derived from the Latin name for red lead, *minium*, which was abundantly used by the medieval illuminators. The term 'portrait miniature' defined a type of painting which is intended to be viewed from a very close range on account of the minuteness of its technique rather than because of its small size. Miniatures can differ immensely in size, from those painted for finger rings, which may be no more than 1 cm (½ in) in height, to large full-length or group portraits which may be as much as 60 cm (24 in) in their larger dimension.

CATEGORIES OF PORTRAIT MINIATURES

Miniatures in oil

These were normally painted on a metal ground, such as copper or silver, in much finer techniques than those usually employed in oil painting. They are normally small, between 3 and 7 cm (1 and 3 in) in height, and date from the sixteenth to the early eighteenth centuries.

Miniatures in enamel

Of all miniatures these are the most stable, being painted in metallic oxides over a white enamel ground laid on a metal base, and then fired at high temperatures. They are invariably slightly convex, and have a glossy surface. Under normal conditions they are very stable, but rapid fluctuations of temperature can cause separation of the enamel from its metal base and the enamel, being brittle, cannot withstand severe physical shocks. A further problem which sometimes arises with enamels on copper or brass plates is that acidity can cause verdigris to form on the metal, and this can gradually throw off the enamel coating.

Miniatures painted in water-colour on vellum

These can usually be recognized by their very matt paint surfaces and by the fact that this technique was restricted to the early years of portrait miniatures, that is from *c*. 1530 to *c*. 1720.

The attachment of water-colour paint to vellum is better than that of water-colour to ivory, and the drier nature of the paint renders it less susceptible to mould growths. Vellum is more flexible than ivory, and is thus better able to adapt itself to changes of temperature and humidity, but in too dry an atmosphere the vellum may warp and separate from its card support.

Miniatures painted in water-colour on ivory

In the early eighteenth century ivory was substituted for vellum as the most common support for miniature painting. It is often difficult to distinguish early-eighteenth-century examples from those painted on vellum, as at first the techniques of applying and mixing the paint were virtually the same as those used for painting on vellum. Towards the end of the eighteenth century, however, much more gum was added to the pigments, making them more transparent and glossy, and this trend continued in the nineteenth century, to the extent that many water-colour miniatures of that period were so heavily gummed that they appear to have been varnished.

In the 1830s a machine was patented which could cut thin slivers of ivory from the circumference of the tusk and these were then flattened to produce sheets of ivory of very large dimensions; full-length and group portraits of 60 cm (24 in) or more in their greater dimension were not uncommon at that period.

Ivory is extremely sensitive to changes in humidity, and a very dry atmosphere can cause it to warp or crack in the direction of its grain and become very brittle. Gum arabic is hygroscopic and in conditions of high humidity it can become sticky and also attract mould growths. The adhesion between water-colour and ivory is not good and in very dry conditions it is common for the paint to flake away from the ivory.

DISPLAY

Light, temperature and relative humidity

The light falling on the miniature should not exceed a maximum of 50 lux with a relative humidity of 55 per cent, while the temperature should not exceed 15°C (60°F).

Central heating, although it may produce a constant temperature, is dangerous because it tends to make the atmosphere too dry.

Cabinets and display cases

Collections of miniatures are best housed in cabinets with drawers or in display cases with covers (see Display cases, p. 231). The pigments of water-colour miniatures are frequently extremely sensitive to light and should where possible be kept covered except when being looked at. Subdued artificial light is preferable to daylight. Make sure that all cabinets, drawers and cases are kept locked.

Hanging

Miniatures should never be hung near fireplaces or radiators, where there may be draughts, or where sunlight will travel across them during the course of the day. Avoid exterior walls which are subject to condensation. There should always be a small gap between the frame and the wall to allow a free passage of air around the miniature.

Where possible, it is safest to hang a group of miniatures in a shadow box, or hanging display case, as the fixing on the frame of the miniature is weaker than any security screw.

STORAGE AND TRANSPORT

Protect miniatures by wrapping them loosely in crumpled acid-free tissue paper. *Never* use cotton wool, cloth or other hygroscopic material. Loosely wrapped tissue paper not only protects the miniatures but allows air to circulate around them.

A useful material for temporary packing for transport is plastic bubble-wrap with air bubbles about 1 cm (½ in) in diameter. This should not be used for permanent storage as it is not inert.

CLEANING

No attempt should be made to clean the frames or lockets of miniature paintings with proprietary metal cleaners. The effect of capillary action can draw such mixtures into the frame and the solvents and reagents used in such cleaners could cause corrosion of metal supports and damage to painted surfaces. For the same reason household glass cleaners should not be used to clean the cover glasses of miniatures. If it is necessary to clean the outside of a cover glass, then it should be carefully wiped with a soft, dry chamois leather. If necessary the glass may be *very* gently breathed upon during the process.

INSPECTION

It is essential that collections of miniatures should be examined at frequent intervals to ensure that they are free of the ailments to which they are commonly prone. Water-colour miniatures are the most vulnerable, and it is fortunate that in this case it is possible to observe and recognize potential dangers long before corrective treatment becomes urgently necessary.

On no account should any attempt be made to open the miniature frame, or to carry out any sort of treatment and, in fact, most of the lockets and frames designed to contain miniatures are impossible to open unless one has professional knowledge and experience.

Miniatures in water-colour

Support

Note any warping or distortion in vellum and ivory miniatures because distortion of the vellum support can lead to flake losses of the paint layer; such movements eventually crack ivory.

Mould

Look for signs of mould growth, especially on miniatures in water-colour on ivory. Mould is usually evident, in the early stage, as white hairy deposits on the paint surface, or as yellowish, raised spots. Such growths eventually cause damage to the paint layer.

Condensation

A further phenomenon, which may be evident in either vellum or ivory miniatures, is the formation of minute droplets of moisture on the inside surface of the cover glass. Check for these by tilting the miniature so that the light is at an acute angle to its surface, and if condensation is observed inform a conservator without delay.

Sulphation

Another disfiguring phenomenon to which miniatures in water-colour are prone is the blackening of lead whites caused by the action of atmospheric hydrogen sulphide.

Miniatures in enamel or oil

Support

It is essential that regular examinations are made to ensure that corrosion of the metal surfaces is not causing separation of the enamel or paint layer. Verdigris can usually be seen as a green deposit round the edge of the painting.

·✤ WATER-COLOURS, DRAWINGS AND PRINTS ✤·

There are many different types of works of art on paper found in historic houses: water-colours, drawings, prints, photographs, maps, plans and documents. Some will be framed, others stored in drawers or kept in albums, boxes and portfolios.

PAPER SUPPORT

Paper was invented in China at the beginning of the second century AD and was first made from a mixture of rags, hemp, fish nets and mulberry bark. By AD 300 paper was generally accepted in China as a substitute for wood, silk or bamboo supports, and by AD 700 sizing techniques were used to improve the surface of the paper for accepting inks. In Europe, the earliest date for the use of gelatine size on paper is about 1337. Although the first papermill was not established in England until 1495, by 1666 the use of paper was so widespread that there was a decree prohibiting the use of linen and cotton for the burial of the dead in order to reserve more of those materials for the paper-makers.

Paper made from linen and cotton rags was strong and durable. It had no chemical additives other than beneficial alkalis such as calcium carbonate introduced fortuitously from hard water or stone grinding machinery. Atmospheric pollution was minimal until the ninteenth century.

Many of the factors which would eventually cause problems for the preservation of paper were introduced after 1760. These included the use of 'loading' agents to improve the surface texture of the paper, such as lead white, plaster of Paris and later China clay; the discovery of chlorine, a strong bleaching agent later used to whiten paper pulps; and the use of rosin as a sizing agent. In the nineteenth century the introduction of paper pulps made from materials other than rags, such as wood and plant fibres, and the manufacturers' attempts to meet the demands for special types of paper, led to a general decline in quality. This problem was aggravated by atmospheric pollution from industrial developments.

The combination of these may produce, for example, paper made from wood treated with bleaches, sized with rosin, loaded with lead white to give a high surface gloss and then exposed to industrial pollution; this gives an idea of the problems which the paper conservator needs the training to detect and the skill to handle.

ARTISTS' MATERIALS

Even with the advent of the commercially successful artists' colourmen in the late seventeenth century, artists continued to mix their own materials from dry pigments and a variety of binding media. This is true of almost all works of art in ink, water-colour, chalk and pastel before *c.* 1830.

Water-colours, gouache

Painting in water-colours became something of an English speciality and developed into a separate genre. In the eighteenth and nineteenth centuries water-colours were produced in great numbers by painters and amateurs of varying accomplishment.

In dry conditions, gum arabic will crack and flake off, often taking the pigment and paper surface with it. In wet conditions, it will attract and

48. A water-colour of the North Gallery at Petworth by Mrs Percy Wyndham, about 1860, showing the upper register of pictures canted out from the walls

encourage mould growths. Honey, which is hygroscopic and encourages mould, was often added to water-colour pigments to keep them moist. Lead white or pigments mixed with lead white will react with hydrogen sulphide in the air and blacken. This is a chemical change which in most cases can be reversed by the paper conservator.

Water-colours will fade quickly and irreversibly if blinds are not kept down and artificial light sources kept below 50 lux. *Never* use a picture light on framed water-colours or hang them directly above table lamps. Display-case lighting should be checked by an expert. Treat the windows of the room with ultraviolet filter varnish or film. When a room is not in use, light should be excluded from water-colours by placing the frame face down on a table, after protecting the surface with a dust-sheet. Or suspend a piece of thick, dark cloth over the front of the frame, which is left hanging on the wall.

Paintings in gouache are essentially water-colour pigments mixed with white body-colour and have a dull, chalk-like surface which is prone to flaking. *Never* touch the surface because grease and moisture leave irreversible stains.

Drawings

Ink drawings

There are four types of ink most commonly used by artists: carbon-black, iron-gall, bistre and sepia. Carbon-black inks were prepared by the ancient Egyptians and Chinese. Iron-gall inks were produced by a chemical reaction from mixing gall inks with ferrous sulphate. Galls are formed on oak trees at punctures made by gall wasps, and contain concentrations of tannic and gallic acids. Iron-gall inks are extremely acidic and some iron-gall ink drawings now have a lace-like appearance where the chemicals in the ink have attacked and destroyed the paper below the pen strokes. Bistre is a brown ink prepared by extracting soluble tars from wood soot; and sepia, made from the ink sacs of cuttlefish, squid and octopus, was widely used for drawings and washes in the nineteenth century.

Inks are especially sensitive to light and will fade irreversibly in even a short period of time. Do not touch the surface of ink drawings, as moisture can reactivate the ink and so cause smearing.

Chalk, pastel and crayon

A few coloured earths were useful to the artist. Natural red chalk was important as a drawing medium in the fifteenth and sixteenth centuries. Black chalk made up of carbon and clay was gradually replaced by graphite pencils. Two varieties of natural white chalk, calcite and soapstone, were used to heighten modelling.

The interest in pastel painting in the eighteenth century led to the preparation of papers with textured grounds, and to the use of other supports, such as vellum, taffeta and linen, roughened with pumice or covered with a coat of glue on to which marble dust or pumice had been sifted.

Binding media included gum arabic, gum tragacanth, sugar candy, milk, whey, beer, glue, stale size, honey, starch and plaster of Paris. As most artists' pigments, including white, could be used to produce pastel sticks, a wide range of colours became possible.

Pastel drawings can be the dimensions of full-length oil portrait paintings, made up of many sheets of paper attached to poor-quality canvas or board. They are particularly prone to mould growths, especially when framed and pressed up against the glass, as was customary. Pastels contain very little binding medium so even small vibrations loosen the adhesion. Pastel and chalk will also smudge and stain irreversibly if the surface is touched. For these reasons, a pastel or chalk drawing should only be removed from its frame by a paper conservator.

Crayons are distinguished from natural or fabricated chalks by the presence of fatty materials in their composition. Experiments with a variety of crayon formulas at the end of the eighteenth century resulted in the invention of lithography, which encouraged the use of crayon by artists for drawings in the nineteenth century.

Prints

Perhaps because prints were produced in greater numbers, they have in general been less well looked after than other works of art on paper. Many houses have fairly extensive collections of prints, often not on show and badly stored.

Prints have from the earliest times been coloured by hand. Attempts were made in the seventeenth and eighteenth centuries to devise methods for printing in colours but these were complicated and the mass production of coloured prints only became widespread in the nineteenth century.

There is a bewildering range of print-making techniques which can be divided into three categories – relief, intaglio and planographic printing.

Relief printing

Relief printing was known to the Chinese well before AD 1000. The image is produced on paper from the inked surface of a block. Lines and areas which are to print black are left raised, while the white areas are cut away. Woodcuts used in European books from the fifteenth century onwards are the most common form of relief printing.

Intaglio printing

Intaglio printing was discovered by metal engravers, who took impressions on dampened paper by rubbing ink into the incised decoration on armour. Engraving on copper plates developed rapidly throughout Europe in the fifteenth century. Great skill was required to engrave the design in reverse on the metal. In the sixteenth century, etching made print-making considerably easier and quicker. The design is scratched with a drawing needle into a wax coating on the plate and relies on the use of acid to bite the design into the metal. Etching produced freer images and was much favoured by artists in the eighteenth and nineteenth centuries. Engravings are characterized by more formal and rigid lines suitable for reproducing paintings. Other intaglio processes include the velvety-black mezzotint and the granular images called aquatints.

All intaglio prints are recognizable from the impression made in the paper by the edge of the metal plate, which is called the plate mark.

Planographic printing

Planographic printing uses a flat printing surface and depends on the anti-pathy of grease and water. Lithography – the original planographic process – was introduced in the last years of the eighteenth century. The design was drawn in greasy crayon on the treated surface of a slab of finely grained limestone; the printing ink adhered to the design but was rejected by the rest of the stone. Lithographic prints have a distinctly flat, surface quality.

CAUSES OF DETERIORATION

Problems common to all works of art on paper may be divided into four categories, as follows.

Acidity

This may be introduced into the paper from either primary or secondary sources.

Primary sources

The addition of chemicals, such as bleach or size, during the manufacture of the paper; the medium of the work – iron-gall ink, lead pigments; atmospheric pollutants such as sulphur dioxide; and exposure to direct or strong light, which will cause oxidization of the cellulose fibres.

Secondary sources

The migration into the paper of acidic by-products from poor-quality mounts and supports, degraded adhesive layers and the backing used in frames such as wood, strawboard and hardboard.

Biological attack

Insect pests

Insects which attack paper are usually feeding on impurities such as sizing agents or the binding media of pigments. Silverfish will follow and eat the ink outlines of prints giving a lace-like appearance to the image and also damaging the paper surface. The common woodworm will eat through paper to find more wood. Thrips (hay bugs) easily get inside frames; once there, their body fluids provide food for mould growths.

Mould

This includes the easily recognizable irregular brown spots known as 'foxing'. Mould growth is encouraged by high relative humidity (over 65 per cent), direct contact of the paper with the glass of the frame and poor ventilation caused by the frame being hung flat against the wall.

Light, temperature and relative humidity

Works of art on paper should ideally be kept below a maximum light level of 50 lux in a temperature of 15°C (60°F), with relative humidity at a constant level between 55 and 65 per cent. Variations in relative humidity will lead to loss of adhesion of the paint, gum and chalk layers, and the eventual disintegration of the image since paper responds quickly to changes in humidity. Even at low light levels, paper will continue to deteriorate as light oxidizes the bonds of the paper fibres and reacts with structural impurities in the paper. Some types of paper, such as those with a high percentage of lignin, are especially sensitive. Such deterioration is progressive and can only be slowed down through careful conservation and improved display or storage conditions. Water-colours, ink drawings and tinted papers are especially sensitive to light.

STORAGE

The room in which works are stored should be clean, dry and well ventilated. Metallic salts in household dust act as a catalyst to chemical change. Water-staining is unsightly and causes wrinkling and curling, which results in loss of pigment. Stagnant air contains high pollution levels, which would accelerate deterioration.

Unframed works

Unframed works are particularly vulnerable to surface abrasion, scratches and loss of paint. An unframed pastel or chalk drawing is most at risk and should be laid face up on clean white blotting paper until a paper conservator can handle the problem.

Unmounted prints, drawings and water-colours should be separated from those which have mounts or backboards, and any which show signs of 'foxing', water-staining or insect attack should be kept separately from those that appear to be in good condition. *Never* store mounted and unmounted works in the same pile and do not mix deteriorating and undamaged works.

An artists' portfolio can be used temporarily for gathering together the unframed works and this will help the conservator to realize the extent of the problem.

49. An example of damage due to variations in relative humidity. The engraving, laid down on canvas, is showing tears and losses due to movement between the paper and the canvas

50. An example of damage due to variations in humidity. The gouache is showing flaking and losses between paint layer and the canvas backing

Interleave the unframed works with acid-free tissue paper and store the portfolio *horizontally*. Do not store the portfolio upright or the contents will slide down, and crease and buckle along the bottom edge.

Hospital portfolios should be marked and kept only for infected paper and should not later be re-used for undamaged work.

Artists' portfolios are not suitable as permanent storage because dust and insects can get in and too much movement can lead to abrasion and surface scratches. Where appropriate, solander boxes of suitable sizes can be ordered in bulk for more permanent storage. The works should be interleaved with acid-free tissue paper and the boxes stored horizontally. Important collections can be stored on mounts of acid-free card in solander boxes measured to the exact size of the mount.

Framed works

Framed works should not be stored for any length of time at floor level where insects and dust can collect and where damage can be caused by cleaning equipment. Simple wooden racks should be made.

Before storing a frame, remove the wire, chain, hooks or rings which could scratch or damage other frames. Protect the frame by interleaving the frames with sheets of corrugated cardboard.

HANGING

Hang the frames whenever possible on an inside wall, where there is no danger of shafts of sunlight passing over the face of the picture. Do not hang immediately above a source of heat, such as a radiator or table lamp. Do not hang near outside doors where light and temperature cannot be controlled.

The darkest wall of the room is usually between the windows and so it is sometimes better to hang water-colours on this outside wall rather than try and reduce the light level of the whole room. Stick corks on the back of the bottom corners of the frame in order to insulate it from the wall and allow air to circulate behind the frame.

The simplest way to hang light frames is to suspend them on rings from two X-picture hooks in the wall. When using picture wire, Aubo Bronze picture line is stronger and longer-lasting than ordinary brass picture wire, the core of which rusts. Never use string. If cord is traditional in a house, use cotton glacie cord. Do not use nylon cord, which looks too modern, stretches and does not dye evenly. (See also Hanging, p. 149.)

CLEANING FRAMES

Any dust which has collected on the top and bottom edges of the frame can be dusted off lightly. Remove dust from gilded surfaces with a ponyhair fitch.

Never polish the glass of a pastel or chalk drawing as static electricity will attract the looser pigment particles on to the inside of the glass, leaving a fuzzy, unfocused image, which cannot be restored.

Never use patent window cleaners or any other liquid, including water, to clean the glass. Buff it up with a soft, clean, dry chamois leather, using a little spit on cotton wool to remove marks such as fly dots. Often the dirt will be found to be on the inside of the glass. Do not unframe the work but leave it to a paper conservator, who will re-set the work correctly in its frame. Avoid rubbing the frame and try protecting the gilded edge by holding a postcard against it when dusting the glass.

ACCIDENTS

If the frame should fall off the wall and the glass break, place the frame face downwards on a flat surface and notify a conservator.

Take care that the bits of glass do not slide around, cutting and abrading the surface of the paper. Do not remove fragments of glass if it is difficult to do so. Correct framing is crucial to the preservation of the work and unfortunately it is as yet only practised by a few specialist framers.

In an emergency, should water get inside a frame, remove the work and lay it face upwards on clean white blotting paper. Do not attempt to remove the print or drawing from its backing or mount and do not heat the room excessively, but let the work dry out slowly. Do not wipe a wet frame or you could remove the gilding.

CONSERVATION

The conservation of paper must take into account all the materials with which the paper comes into contact. The mount and the way the work is framed are important in the preservation of paper. Once a print or drawing has been sealed into its frame, it is impossible to check whether correct methods and materials have been used until signs of deterioration appear. It is therefore essential that a paper conservator should supervise the mount-cutter and framer. It should be remembered that the framer handles the work itself and bad workshop habits or simply lack of available clean surfaces could lead to irreparable damage.

There is little point in re-mounting and re-setting a work correctly in its frame without first checking its condition. Deterioration involving mould growth, and acidic build-up from contact with poor-quality materials, would only contaminate the new environment. There are also technical dangers in the conservation of paper, which are not immediately apparent, such as incorrectly applied and unneutralized chemicals, which can lead to irreparable damage.

·✢ PARCHMENT AND VELLUM ✢·

Prepared animal skins were originally used as a surface for painting and lettering because of their supposed strength and flexibility. Unfortunately, natural ageing of the skin layers and deterioration of the proteins in the chemical structure of the skin lead to brittleness and dimensional instability, which means that the skin will revert to its previous shape and be difficult to flatten.

Coloured pigment and gilding layers are usually inert. The binding media, however, are hygroscopic, and respond quickly to any variations in relative humidity and are subject to oxidation and bacteriological attack.

The wrinkling and cockling of parchment responding to variations in relative humidity will cause the pigment and gilding layers to fracture and flake off.

See also Routine examination, p. 47.

DISPLAY

Do not hang framed parchment or vellum works on exterior walls, near pipework, or by entrance doorways. They should be kept out of direct sunlight or strong artificial light (50 lux maximum with ultraviolet filters where appropriate).

Framed parchment and vellum should not come into contact with the glass as the pigment layers will adhere to it. Contact will also encourage mould growth, which can spread quickly in damp conditions. A paper conservator will arrange for acid-free card window mounts or fillets to be fitted.

Framed parchment testimonials or addresses with seals attached are a specialist problem and should not be unframed without first seeking advice.

Unframed parchment or vellum should be shown to a paper conservator and handled as little as possible. Parchment or vellum should only be unframed by an expert.

Can storied urn or animated bust
Back to its mansion call the fleeting breath?

Thomas Gray,
Elegy Written in a Country Churchyard, 1751

CHAPTER TWELVE

SCULPTURE AND PLASTERWORK

51. A marble statue of a companion of Diana by Claude-Augustin Cayot (1677–1722), on the Borghese balustrade at Cliveden. The statue is now shown indoors

Most historic houses have some structural decoration on the exterior and urns, sculpture or balustrades in the garden. In some there are important marble fireplaces and often busts, statues or decorative plasterwork.

Where collections of classical sculpture exist, in houses open to the public, special efforts should be made to explain its interest and importance so that visitors can understand and enjoy the collection, as this is ultimately the key to its preservation.

CAUSES OF DAMAGE AND DECAY

All materials deteriorate but the common saying 'as hard as rock' leads us to expect stone and marble to be durable. In fact they can easily be damaged by both physical and chemical action, and objects made of stone may be vulnerable because of the way in which they have been put together.

Marble, for example, is made up of masses of crystals and a blow will bruise the surface, causing irreversible disruption of the crystals surrounding the point of impact. Because it is porous, the smoke from a fire can turn it permanently brown or black, and it can also be stained by absorbing colour such as rust and verdigris, stains from mould growths, wine from glasses left on pedestals, or paints and dyes from unsuitable packing materials.

Statues, fireplaces and decorative friezes were made up of various sections joined together by a wide variety of methods and materials; antique marble sculpture, collected on the Grand Tour, often has eighteenth-century additions and restorations to complete the composition. Iron set in some protective coating such as lead or shellac was the metal most commonly used to join pieces. This can vary from large dowels running up the legs and supporting the whole weight of the sculpture, to many small iron pins where corroded surfaces have been patched. Recent repairs where iron cramps have been set in mortars, cements and plasters are likely to cause damage.

Moisture starts off a harmful process of chemical change which attacks glues and metal used in the construction. Internal iron supports will expand as the iron changes to iron oxide (rusts) and this will eventually split the object apart. Changes in temperature and the level of relative humidity in a house may easily cause condensation on the surface of alabaster with potentially disastrous results, since alabaster is soluble in water. The siting of objects can also cause damage. For example, a marble bust should not be placed by an open window in a damp draught, since the moisture would bring out iron-staining and cause permanent discoloration of the surface.

Rain not only wears away the surface of stone and marble, but also, when the atmosphere is polluted by sulphur dioxide, corrodes it chemically. A white crust forms on the surface which 'spalls' away, leaving a roughened area which is quickly blackened by grime and dirt, and the surface continues to corrode away. Not only will carved detail be lost, but water will penetrate in winter; the pockets of water then freeze and expand, causing fracturing and splitting.

The pollution of the atmosphere in Britain is not confined to the towns, but is spread across the countryside as well – indeed we export much of it to Scandinavia, since the prevailing winds blow in from the Atlantic. Experiments have shown that the sulphur dioxide content of the air indoors is about one third of that outside, so even objects indoors are not exempt from this type of attack.

ROUTINE MAINTENANCE

Cleaning should be left to a sculpture conservator, with the exception of routine maintenance which mainly consists in brushing out finely carved mouldings with a white bristle brush (a hogshair fitch) once a year to remove surface dirt. Avoid black bristles which could leave marks on white marble. The brush must be used dry and should be kept scrupulously clean. To prevent the dust from floating all over the room, brush out with one hand while holding a Hoover Dustette in the other so that the dust is sucked up. Use the crevice head bound round with foam rubber and secured with strong adhesive tape so as to protect the sculpture from accidental knocks.

Never dust marble with cloths which smear greasy grime over the surface. Never use feather dusters, which can break and scratch the surface.

Never use any liquid or cleaning packs on sculpture or plasterwork, since alabaster is easily mistaken for marble and painted plaster for terracotta. Marble is porous and any liquid applied to the surface may drive dirt or stains further in. Acids attack marble and remove the surface layers. Alabaster is not porous, but it dissolves in water, so unskilled cleaning could result in the complete loss of surface detail. Plaster may be flaking and would also dissolve in water. In addition there is a danger of water activating harmful salts or the iron which is present in some stone – for example, as iron pyrites – which, in conjunction with water, can cause irreversible staining.

Even fireplaces should not be washed because water, as already explained, is potentially dangerous and washing would not achieve the desired effect. The layer of tarry dirt on fireplaces cannot be reduced or removed safely except by a sculpture conservator, who should undertake a programme of *in situ* cleaning when necessary. When the fireplace is no longer in use the conservator can apply a protective coating after treatment, to help restore the polished finish and inhibit re-soiling from household dirt.

Stains such as ink or lipstick, and the marks made by cigarettes being stubbed out on marble bases or wine glasses being left on stone or marble surfaces, should be left to a sculpture conservator to treat. Tests are carried

52 and 53. Spalling of a Portland stone façade at Castle Coole, caused by the rusting of internal iron cramps

out before the conservator embarks on any cleaning, and the overall effect should be discussed with him, taking into account old restorations and repairs and irreversible damage such as iron-staining, all of which will become more apparent after cleaning.

During cleaning the conservator should also note historical information like tool marks, traces of pigmentation or even signatures, which may be hidden under dirt layers. A photographic and written record should be kept of the presence of iron, and, as a priority, where there is movement, the joints will be separated and refixed. Any filler used will be softer than the sound marble. Conservation methods do not require any mechanical keying or cutting of the surface.

(For routine maintenance of decorative plasterwork, see Decorative carved wood and plasterwork, p. 225)

INSPECTION

While cleaning has, therefore, to be restricted, the task of the sculpture conservator is greatly assisted if during routine dusting a look-out is kept for structural instability and discoloration or flaking of the surface.

Structural instability

The conservator should be informed immediately if anything is loose or unstable – a wobbly pedestal, for example – or where jointing material has dropped out of sections of a fireplace. It will sometimes be found that the surbase or socle, which is the smaller stand that is usually placed on top of a pedestal to serve as the base for a bust or statue, is dowelled neither to the pedestal nor to the bust.

Discoloration of the surface

A brownish discoloration is a fairly certain sign of a rusting iron cramp or dowel and it shows that the process of expansion by rusting has reached the danger point where cracks will soon appear.

Flaking or sugaring of the surface

A painted object should always be inspected for any slight lifting or blistering of the paint surface. Plaster and terracotta sometimes have protective surface coatings or layers which may also begin to flake in the wrong conditions. Marble and stone surfaces were usually smoothly finished or polished. If a surface appears rough or granular, this should be reported, as it may be the beginning of a harmful salt formation caused by air pollution and an incorrect environment. In the case of marble, 'sugaring' usually begins on the underside of any carved area, and this can be detected by rubbing the little finger gently along these undercut areas to check for loose crystals.

HANDLING AND FIXING

Sculpture combines weight with fragility and it is easily scratched or bruised. Even a bust is made up of at least two pieces, more often than not dowelled with iron. Marble can easily be broken in moving by its weight alone. The surface absorbs dirt and grease and it is advisable to wear clean white cotton gloves when handling it.

A sculpture conservator or mason should always advise beforehand and be present when large statues have to be moved, but bad handling can cause damage to smaller objects too. Take a bust lying on its back on a wooden floor: undue pressure would have been put on the socle joint while the bust was being lowered using the edge of the socle as a pivot, and while the bust remained horizontal. White marble would also pick up varnish or wax where it was in contact with the floor.

Sculptured reliefs

The lower edge of sculptured reliefs should be supported on stainless steel brackets, padded with chamois leather.

Marble, terracotta and plaster are not at all flexible. A wooden frame will undergo considerable dimensional change, particularly in a heated room, which could put pressure on the relief and crack it. Allowance must be made for this movement and the fitting of all framed reliefs should be checked by a conservator.

Reliefs should not be fixed above a radiator. Convected warm air passing over the surface of the sculpture will distort a wooden frame as well as depositing dirt on the surface of the relief.

Mortar

Wet mortar should not be used indoors for fixing or repairing, for example, fireplaces. The stone or marble is dry and would absorb the moisture, with the danger of activating dormant salts and affecting old iron dowels. The conservator or recommended mason would use modern, inert adhesives to embed the dowels.

Pedestals and socles

The most vulnerable pedestals are the tall, narrow-based, hollow wooden type. They are usually placed up against a wall for support, but the busts which stand on them are often too deep to allow this. Even when they are flush with a wall, sideways movement is still possible. Stability is best achieved by filling at least the base of the pedestal with clean, dry sand or, if possible, by fitting a collar round the pedestal and fixing it to the wall. If the floor under the pedestal is uneven, a suitable bed should be provided in order

54. A marble bust and pedestal perched precariously on a cracked plinth

to eliminate movement. The use of wedges is not recommended because they are too easily moved by accident or by vibration.

The bust should be dowelled to its socle and the socle to the pedestal. The sculpture conservator will use stainless steel, as iron, bronze, steel and copper all have corrosive properties that would eventually cause staining and disruption.

DECORATORS AND BUILDERS

Move the sculpture out of the room or protect the statue from accidental damage by constructing a strong wooden box around it. Nothing – brooms, ladders, hands, elbows – should ever be leaned against sculpture.

TEMPORARY PACKING FOR TRANSPORT

A thick layer of polystyrene pellets at least 5 cm (2 in) deep is one of the safest ways of supporting sculpture in a crate. The pellets can be re-used. Foam rubber, 1–5 cm (½–2 in) thick, can be used as a substitute for the pellets. The strong wooden crate should be screwed together, not nailed. The sculpture should first be wrapped in polythene bags, sheeting, or acid-free tissue paper. *Never* wrap marble in coloured materials or baize. If there were the slightest moisture, the colour would be absorbed by the marble.

STORAGE

Stone, marble, terracotta and so forth should be stored with the same care and attention as other more apparently fragile materials. Provided the storage is dry, outhouses and garages may be suitable, but only if the space is uncluttered and set aside for sculpture. Damp cellars must not be used and the temperature of the store should not drop below 5°C (41°F) or rise above 15°C (60°F); the relative humidity should be between 50 and 60 per cent.

As a precaution against rising damp, keep the sculpture clear of the ground by placing it on a wooden palette or, if this is not possible, on clean polythene sheeting. *Never* stand white marble on a carpet or on a polished floor, either of which could stain the marble. Cover the sculpture loosely with a dust-sheet. Do not cover with polythene, which could cause condensation.

Enough space should be allowed so that each piece can be inspected and so that there is no danger of one object knocking against another.

Any fragments or pieces that may have been accidentally knocked off, however small, should be saved and kept in a cardboard box, protected by crumpled acid-free tissue paper. Do not use newspaper, which is very acidic. Do not keep fragments in paper or polythene bags. Place a note in the box identifying the broken piece.

55 and 56. Italian Renaissance well-heads at Cliveden as normally shown and (below) under protective covers for the winter

GARDEN SCULPTURE AND ORNAMENTS

A photographic record of garden sculpture and ornaments is highly desirable so that signs of deterioration can be monitored. Black-and-white photographs are more suitable for detecting cracks and repairs, while colour shows surface changes, such as the spread of iron-staining or the growth of algae. Regular inspections can be made to check the speed of degradation against good photographs.

In the meantime any programme of repair and conservation undertaken by a mason must be tackled with the advice of a sculpture conservator, because there is no point in dealing with a plinth which is out of alignment if the foundation on which it stands is inadequate. In most cases a concrete raft exceeding the width of the plinth is needed and the base should be separated from the plinth by a damp-proof membrane, because the moisture drawn up by capillary action from the ground contains harmful salts.

A space around the base of the plinth should be dug and filled with pebbles to improve drainage and it should be kept clear of grass and plants, so that there is less likelihood of the base being knocked by the grass cutter. Overhanging greenery should be trimmed back because a dripping, damp atmosphere encourages the growth of algae. Ivy must not be allowed to climb up a plinth because it feeds on moisture and will break down the surface of stone and marble.

Winter covers for garden sculpture should be placed in position in dry weather no later than October. Ventilation should be incorporated into the design to allow the residual moisture in the sculpture to dry out and to prevent damp being trapped inside the box. The design should also include fixing posts to prevent wind knocking the box against the sculpture.

Never use straw and canvas tied to the sculpture with ropes. This method does protect sculpture from freezing but it retains moisture, which promotes the growth of destructive soluble salts. There is also the danger of staining from straw, canvas or tarpaulin and the use of ropes, year after year, abrades fragile surfaces and leaves patches of rubbed stone.

Stone and marble

Stone or marble vases and urns are a pleasing feature of many gardens, and some of these have very high quality relief decorations. More rare are urns of bronze, copper or lead. These vases or urns were occasionally designed to be planted and they have a hole somewhere near the base for draining off water. In the past they were usually provided with metal liners for holding the earth and protecting the material of which they were made. Liners can now be made of fibreglass and any ornament with plants in it should be provided with a liner to protect it from the corrosive action of earth, decaying vegetation, and fertilizers. The ornament should also be provided with a means of drainage if possible.

Lead

Garden statuary and urns were frequently made of lead and many eighteenth-century examples are of high artistic quality. The lead was usually painted white to simulate marble, or stone coloured, or bronze coloured. The paint had the additional virtue of protecting the lead from atmospheric corrosion.

Lead sculptures normally have an iron armature or skeleton which supports the weight internally, and sculptures and urns often have iron pins or dowels. The iron corrodes and loses its supportive strength over the years and it must be replaced by stainless steel.

Unstable plinths are often a problem since if the plinth is not level it puts an uneven strain on the sculpture erected upon it.

Late nineteenth- and twentieth-century examples of lead work produced by slush casting are usually not of very high quality and, in view of the high cost of lead repairs, a replacement may be preferable.

Earlier examples of fine craftsmanship should be inspected by a specialist in the conservation of lead sculpture.

Old lead water cisterns frequently have pleasing decorative mouldings and their date of manufacture on them, and are frequently used as garden ornaments. They should be raised off the ground on a grid of flat stones or slate with the gaps between the supports sufficiently close to prevent the lead from sagging. It is better not to fill a cistern with earth and plant it since the strain will eventually fracture it and there will be a steady corrosive action from earth, decaying vegetation, and fertilizers. If the cistern is planted, it should have a fibreglass liner and drainage holes with pipes going through the base of the liner and the lead so that water does not rest on the bottom of the cistern.

MAKING CASTS

Few methods are not damaging to the surface of the original, and before a cast is taken the statue or carving should be inspected and prepared by the sculpture conservator and not by the cast-maker.

There is a fine stuffed chavender
A chavender, or chub.
That decks the rural pavender,
The pavender, or pub.
Wherein I eat my gravender,
My gravender, or grub.

W. St Leger
The Chavender, or Chub

TAXIDERMY

57. Big game trophies in the Tenants' Hall at Tatton Park

·�֍ TAXIDERMY ✤·

The present laws relating to the hunting of depleted or rare species mean that historic houses may possess many irreplaceable natural-history specimens. Every collection should be catalogued by a specialist who can identify the rare or now extinct specimens, which should only be touched by a recommended taxidermist.

DISPLAY

Butterflies, moths and insects should be kept in drawers or under glass, and small creatures in glass cases, to prevent contamination from dust or general handling. The larger animals in a house open to the public should be removed from areas where they could be touched by visitors.

All natural-history specimens are as sensitive to light and as susceptible to mould and insect attack as textiles and water-colours. Specimens should therefore be displayed out of direct light at a maximum level of 50 lux. Glass cases should have covers made of a dense material such as velvet which can be used to exclude all light when the house is closed. The temperature should be as even as possible at about 15°C (60°F) and 55 per cent relative humidity. If the conditions are too dry the skins of stuffed creatures become very brittle and crack, and seams split; if the conditions are too damp, wires inside the body can rust, especially the legs of birds, which may collapse and fall off their perches. If the conditions are too damp and warm, mould may grow, particularly round the eyes and beak.

Acid attacks the structural components of eggs and shells and so it is particularly important that acid-free materials are used where birds' eggs and shells are stored or displayed (see Display cases, p. 231).

INSECT ATTACK

The greatest danger common to all natural-history specimens is attack by insects. Few display cases are well sealed and thus butterflies and moths stored in drawers and animals and birds in glass cases are very vulnerable, as infestation may proceed unnoticed. Moth and carpet beetle are the chief pests, and can ruin and even destroy a specimen.

Protection and treatment

In bad cases of infestation involving many specimens expert advice must be sought. Old birds' nests on buildings should be removed from eaves and chimneys as they provide a haven and breeding ground for a variety of insect pests that attack objects in houses.

Do not introduce a new specimen into a collection without first checking it very carefully for signs of insect attack.

Butterflies and moths

Moth-balls can be used as a temporary preventive measure. Advice must be sought for more permanent protection.

When an attack is confirmed, place the drawer and its contents in a plastic bag with a strip of Vapona or Mafu. Close the bag tightly and leave for four to six weeks; then open it in a well-ventilated room or outside in the fresh air, as these concentrated fumes can be toxic to humans.

Birds and animals

Careful examination should be made at least once a year for signs of insect attack. Falling hair or feathers are a sign of deterioration. The pads of animals are a favourite place for moths to breed, and should be examined thoroughly.

When specimens are displayed in glass cases examine the case carefully and if it is sealed do not disturb. If there is evidence of dust in the case, indicating that insects may have got in, place a small pile of naphtha or paradichlorobenzene flakes behind a rock or piece of bark as a preventive measure. Then seal the case immediately with a water-based paper tape. Do not use masking tape or Sellotape, as these dry out and lift away from their adhesive layer.

When the attack is confined to one or two birds or animals, seal the affected specimens in an airtight container, such as a plastic bag, in which some Vapona or Mafu strips have been placed. The number of strips will vary according to the size of the animal (a specimen the size of a fox would need six strips). Leave for four to six weeks and then open the container in the fresh air (see above).

Fish

Fish are very difficult to prepare for display. Traces of fat are left within the skin and body which sometimes appear as drops of grease under the fish. When this happens, beware of the bacon beetle. If there is evidence of attack, an expert must be consulted.

CLEANING

All cleaning should be kept to a minimum and should take place when the specimens are examined for insect attack. Free-standing specimens will need cleaning more frequently than those protected by glass.

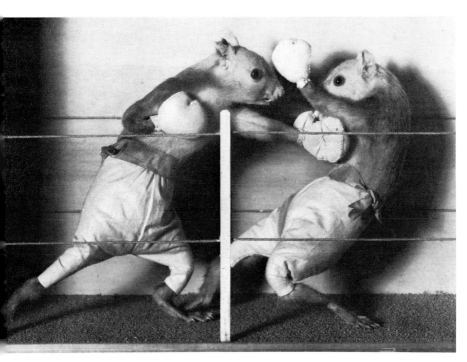

58. Boxing squirrels. One of a collection of tableaux at Castle Ward in which squirrels are 'set up' and are engaged in human activities

When cleaning, isolate the specimen from the rest of the collection so that if insects are discovered they will not be brushed off near other specimens and so contaminate them.

Animals

Always test for moulting by brushing an area over a piece of paper. If there is no sign of loose hair, blow (not suck) with an Electrolux 350E at its lowest power and then rearrange the fur by combing gently using a plastic comb with wide-spaced teeth. A gentle stroke of the hand can give back a little shine but this must be kept to a minimum – on no account add any oil.

When there is a trace of moulting but no sign of insect attack an expert must be consulted as the skin may have been badly cured, which can result in the animal becoming bald in patches or even completely bald.

59. A picturesque caseful of curiosities collected by the Yorke family at Erddig, posing particular problems for the conservator

Ears

Be very careful of ears, as they are fragile and can tear easily.

Eyes, teeth and hooves

Take a tiny swab of cotton wool wrapped round a pair of tweezers or a wooden cuticle-stick and just dampened with methylated spirits, and quickly wipe the eyes, teeth and hooves. Be careful not to touch the surrounding skin as the methylated spirits can take off the colour.

Noses

Dust with a clean, dry duster or hogshair fitch brush. If the nose is very dry, consult a taxidermist.

Antlers and horns

Antlers with rough surfaces can be dusted with a hogshair fitch brush; smooth antlers with a soft, clean duster.

Lions

Lions can have their manes brushed with a soft brush but be very careful of the ears, which can tear easily.

Elephants and rhinoceroses

Brush with a 5 cm (2 in) wide paint-brush, while at the same time using a Hoover Dustette fitted with the crevice tool in order to collect the dust.

Birds

Taxidermists use a bird's wing, with feathers, for brushing dust off specimen birds. After brushing, the feathers can be rearranged with a needle or a pair of very pointed tweezers.

Birds' eggs

Dust only with a soft cloth or ponyhair fitch brush. *Never* use water or any other liquid as the colour may come off.

Butterflies and moths

Never touch the specimens; if the bottom of a drawer or board holding them becomes dusty, brush carefully with a ponyhair or hogshair fitch brush. The glass cover may need cleaning occasionally with a dry chamois leather. Do not get water or any other liquid near the specimens.

Shells

Dust with a soft, clean duster or a hogshair fitch brush. If very dirty, shells can be washed with water to which a drop of Synperonic N has been added. Rinse and dry well. A hair-dryer set at cool could be useful here. However great care must be taken when washing spiral shells to prevent water getting inside, or the desiccated remains of the creature, which are often still inside these shells, will start decomposing and smell vile. Bivalves such as mussels, clams, etc., are easy to wash as the dead mollusc has been removed.

... there was sweete tapestry hangings with small figures and very much silk, they look'd as fresh as if new tho' bought severall yeares ...

Celia Fiennes at Chatsworth, 1697

I chose my wife, as she did her wedding gown, not for a fine glossy surface, but such qualities as would wear well.

Goldsmith, The Vicar of Wakefield, 1766

We'd take all the carpets up and take them up on Cage Hill in a pony cart and beat them. There'd be twenty odd fellows up there beating, brushing, sweeping the carpets. The housemaids beat the carpets? No. We used to beat the housemaids.

Harry Jackson ... at Lyme Park,
from Kedrun Laurie, Cricketer Preferred

TEXTILES

60. The state bed and accompanying seat furniture made for James II, at Knole

·✤ TEXTILES ✤·

Textiles are made to be handled – curtains to be drawn, upholstery sat on and carpets walked on – and it is a natural impulse to want to feel what a material is made of; but when many thousands of people visit a historic house every year, they can cause a lot of wear and damage even to new textiles. Most visitors will curb the instinct to touch if this is explained to them, but the siting of objects can help avoid unnecessary wear.

Siting of objects

Some irreversible damage from light is unavoidable unless textiles are stored in total darkness but it is sometimes possible to place vulnerable objects in a darker part of the room.

Make sure that furniture is not pushed up against textiles – a chair against a wall, a sofa table biting into the back of a sofa or furniture against tapestries.

In houses open to the public, watch visitors in crowded rooms and notice the textiles which are constantly rubbed or touched. If, for example, people lean on the back of a chair to peer at a photograph, it may be possible to re-site the photograph or move the chair.

Make it the responsibility of the room steward to see that information bats are not put down on upholstered chairs or stools. In selecting a suitable place, remember that these bats can scratch polished wood and also marble.

Use of ropes

Bed hangings can be roped off but it is still necessary to have a steward in the room when a house is open to the public. In the past, visitors have reached over the rope and damaged hangings while the part of the bed out of reach has remained in good condition.

Where stanchions and ropes are used to protect a carpet, remember that visitors walk right up to the rope so the stanchions must stand well back on the drugget to prevent feet wearing the carpet along the line of the rope. Do not stand a stanchion directly on the carpet or it will leave a mark.

When ropes are used to stop visitors sitting on chairs tie them loosely so as not to cut into the upholstery.

Carpets and rugs

All carpeting is expensive to replace and some is irreplaceable. Most carpets and rugs are walked on occasionally and carpeting along the route which visitors follow in a house open to the public takes an enormous amount of wear.

Carpet paper

A thick type of brown paper placed between the floor and underlay can protect the carpet from rising damp, prevent dust rising from between the floor boards and stop the underlay from marking the wooden floor.

Underlay

A good underlay greatly prolongs the life of a carpet. It reduces wear by taking up the unevenness of the floor. The underlay should come to the edge of the carpet. Never overlap or turn back underlay as this makes the surface uneven.

The International Wool Secretariat recommends the use of hairfelt under-lay of contract quality. Some other types deteriorate so badly that the underlay sticks to the wooden floor. Do not use foam rubber or composition-backed underlays which deteriorate unevenly or those with a dimpled surface which could cause uneven wear. On stone floors and other places where underfelt could absorb damp, carpet paper should be laid under the felt.

Druggets

It is known from old records that coverings or druggets were supplied with carpets to give protection from dirt, light and wear, and were used to protect a good carpet except when it was uncovered for state occasions. Nowadays no antique carpet should be walked on by visitors to a historic house, but where this is unavoidable, it can be protected with a drugget, particularly in doorways and where visitors are channelled round a corner. As some drug-gets at present in use are doing more harm than good, research and experi-ments have been carried out with the help of the International Wool Secre-tariat (see Appendix 2, p. 247).

Turning and moving carpets

Carpets and rugs wear more evenly if turned round every year. Stair-carpets should be moved a few inches periodically by a professional carpet-layer, renewing the underlay on the treads where necessary.

61. Small wooden discs placed beneath the legs of furniture to protect valuable carpets

If a carpet is too large for a room, do not turn it under, as great damage can be caused along the fold. Roll the spare carpet on to a roller right side outside so as to prevent any creases forming (see also To roll a carpet, p. 211).

Castors on furniture

Protect carpets by placing small discs under the legs of heavy furniture, especially when it is fitted with metal castors. The discs can be made of three-ply wood and coloured to blend in with the carpet.

Table carpets

The edges of tables should be well padded out with old blankets or something similar before a table carpet is placed in position. Sharp corners cut into the fibres and cause damage. When a house is closed for the winter, table carpets should be taken off and laid flat on the floor or rolled up right side outside (see To roll a carpet, p. 211). If this is not done the carpet will take up the shape of the table and the strain could start splits along the folds.

62 and 63. A conversation group, by J. H. Mortimer (1741–79), showing chairs and a settee with case covers in use and (below) an armchair at Petworth, with case cover copying those in the Mortimer picture

Case covers and dust-sheets

Use of dust-sheets to cover upholstered furniture when a house is closed reduces the damage from light and dust. (See Appendix 3, Dust-sheets and winter covers, p. 250.) Faded colours and brittle materials can never be restored to their original condition.

Even when the house is open, consider fitting all but one of a set of chairs with case covers. Great care must be taken when putting covers on and taking them off. Measuring for case covers should be left to a textile conservator as, if they are too tight, damage can be done to the textile underneath and the case cover will do more harm than good.

Curtains

During the months when the house is closed, release curtains from tie-backs and draw them slightly to relax the folds. The bottom of heavy curtains should be folded into three and lifted neatly over the back of a chair or on to the windowsill so as to take some weight off the rest of the curtain and allow creases to relax out.

Festoon or draw curtains should be let down during the winter to release the folds.

CLEANING

Never attempt to wash or dry-clean textiles of any historic importance without first consulting a textile conservator.

The safest way to remove dust and dirt from textiles is by vacuuming. As textiles should be handled as little as possible leave tapestries and curtains for a year or so and limit day-to-day cleaning to the carpets that are walked on.

It is essential to look at the whole of a textile before vacuuming. If it is very fragile, leave it strictly alone until the next visit of a textile conservator. *Never* vacuum embroideries which have beads or sequins as the suction will remove any which are loose. The vacuum cleaner has also taken its toll of seventeenth- and eighteenth-century fringes.

Equipment should be suitable for the job, not only for the safety of the textile but also to save time. The general-purpose head should always be used unless otherwise specified. *Never* use brush attachments when cleaning textiles, as brushes of any description can rough up loose threads.

Vacuum equipment and its uses

Most large houses will need three different vacuum cleaners (see Appendix 3, Electrical equipment, p. 249).

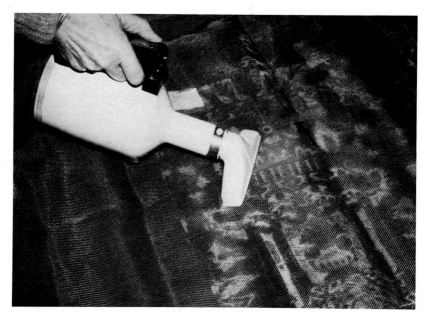

64. Vacuuming fragile textiles with a Hoover Dustette and protective nylon screening

Hoover Dustette

A small hand-held vacuum cleaner, ideal for most textiles, including tapestries, upholstery and fragile carpets. The set of attachments is sold separately but is essential for the proper use of this machine. Use the flexible hose for better control. When vacuuming large areas the Dustette can be hung from the shoulder or tied to the waist.

Electrolux 350E

This is a cylinder vacuum cleaner, with variable suction and flexible hose. For stronger textiles such as antique carpets and rugs which are in good condition, use the suction at medium or low depending on the strength of the carpet and how dirty it is. The long flexible hose makes the 350E ideal for stair-carpets.

Industrial vacuum

Never use an industrial vacuum on any textile except modern carpeting. It is suitable for druggets as it has a large head which covers the ground quickly.

Nylon screening

This screening is used with the Hoover Dustette and Electrolux 350 E to prevent the textile from being sucked into the nozzle of the vacuum; it holds down any loose threads and protects fringes.

On flat horizontal surfaces the vacuum head should glide over the nylon screening and must not be pressed down as this could cause damage without increasing the amount of dirt removed. Remember that it is the suction which removes the dirt. The nylon mesh is soft and pliable but heavy enough not to be sucked up by the vacuum. The sharp edges of the screening must be bound with tape, and the net should be washed frequently.

On vertical or shaped surfaces it is easier to use the crevice vacuum head covered in soft nylon net held in position by a strong elastic band.

Carpets and rugs

Dust and grit cause great damage so carpets that are walked on should be vacuumed daily, even though this will inevitably remove fibres.

Fragile carpets must not be walked on and should only be vacuumed once or twice a year using the Hoover Dustette with protective nylon screening. The knotted type of carpet fringe is particularly vulnerable. Protect the fringe with nylon screening and use the Hoover Dustette.

Never attempt any washing or dry-cleaning of carpets or rugs without first consulting a textile conservator. Some commercial cleaning methods accelerate re-soiling.

Upholstery

Care should be taken when dusting chairs, etc., that the duster does not come into contact with any part of the textile. Special care should be taken of fringes. Drop-in chair seats should be removed before dusting, especially when polish is applied to the wood.

Upholstery in good condition can be gently patted with a plastic fly swat to loosen the dirt before using the Hoover Dustette fitted with the general-purpose or crevice attachment. Where conditions in a house are very dusty, upholstery may need to be vacuumed more than once a year so that it does not become impregnated with dust.

Old and fragile upholstery should always be protected by nylon screening while vacuuming.

Moth can attack the stuffing of an upholstered chair, so the spaces down the back and sides of the seat should be carefully vacuumed using the crevice head.

Hangings

As textiles should be handled as little as possible only vacuum fragile curtains and tapestries once every few years. In this way it is possible to deal with one or two rooms of a large house every winter.

Curtains, bed hangings

Always lift the end of floor-length curtains on to a chair or windowsill before polishing or washing the floor.

Pelmets and valances should not be taken down but vacuumed with the Hoover Dustette. On vertical and shaped surfaces use the Hoover Dustette with the crevice tool covered in soft nylon net, which can be held in position by a strong elastic band.

Bed hangings or curtains which are strong enough can be taken down and vacuumed flat on a large table using the Hoover Dustette and protecting the textile with nylon screening. The textile can then be folded into three lengthwise, with the folds well padded with acid-free tissue paper, and wrapped in a dust-sheet for the winter while the rest of the room is thoroughly spring-cleaned.

Tapestries

Handle as little as possible and report all new splits and deterioration to a textile conservator.

It is better to leave some dust than to over-insist and agitate a weak place. *Never* use a stronger suction than the Hoover Dustette. Use the crevice head covered in nylon net if the tapestry is in good condition. Float it over the entire surface without touching the tapestry. If the tapestry is very fragile consult a conservator.

Tapestry chairs and other flat surfaces can be protected with nylon screening, and vacuumed with the Hoover Dustette, using the general-purpose attachment.

Banners and flags

These are often extremely fragile; they should be left hanging and not touched in any way unless otherwise advised by a textile conservator.

Embroideries

Handle as little as possible. Do not touch intricate embroideries such as stump work or gold work without seeking expert advice.

65. The state bed at Clandon, with case curtains half pulled, and a light frame to protect the elaborate armchair *en suite*

Most embroideries can be vacuumed with the Hoover Dustette, first protecting the surface with nylon screening. *Never* vacuum embroideries which have beads or sequins as the suction will remove any which are loose.

REPAIRS

When dealing with important or fragile textiles, do not attempt repairs of any kind without first consulting a qualified textile conservator.

Always sew and *never* use commercial adhesives on textiles. They can harden and discolour and are often impossible to remove.

Upholstery and hangings can be enormously improved by sewing down loose braid, cord or gimp.

Netting

Net can keep in place damaged and deteriorating textiles, but netting should only be considered as a holding operation until the textile can be properly restored or renewed.

Net can trap dust and dirt and is also abrasive so only the finest and softest should be used. It should be dyed to the background colour of the textile.

The placing on of the net and the sewing down can cause more damage to silk and braid than if they had been left alone.

On curtains, net can balloon out and look unsightly. It must be taken up to the curtain heading; if this is not done the curtain is liable to tear lower down where it has been perforated by the sewing on of the net.

Always consult a textile conservator before starting to net.

Linings

Most hanging textiles such as curtains, bed hangings and tapestries have linings or bound edges which may shrink in time. The way the textile hangs is then distorted and damage can occur along the creases. If the hangings are in good condition release the lining or edging – this should remove the cockling and allow the textile to hang straight once again. Do not touch anything fragile as in some cases it is only the lining which is keeping the textile together.

Fixings

All fixings should be examined when vacuuming the hangings; missing rings and hooks should be replaced. Where a textile hangs straight on a wall, Velcro or a batten in a sleeve should be used for hanging so that there is no strain at any one point. Consult a conservator before altering the hanging as damage could be done in taking the textile down.

PESTS AND MOULD

The common clothes moth, brown house moth and carpet beetle do the greatest damage to textiles. The best protection against these is thorough dusting and vacuum cleaning. If they are found, a textile conservator will advise on the correct treatment.

Moths

The larva stage, which does the damage, can last for several months. Moths like to lay their eggs in enclosed spaces beneath heavy furniture, the inside of a drawer which may be slightly damp or the felt of card tables. The larvae feed on wool and other animal fibres.

Carpet beetle

Dirt and darkness attract the carpet beetle. At least once a year all woollen materials, including carpets and rugs, should be inspected carefully over their entire surface for signs of infestation even if this involves moving heavy furniture. The 'woolly bear', as the insect is called in its early stages, is far more active than a moth grub, so look out for holes scattered over a wide area. Care should be taken to vacuum thoroughly along the borders of carpets and under furniture.

Mould

The treatment of mould should be left to an expert. Check the temperature and humidity of the room and consult a conservator.

66. A rare seventeenth-century X-frame stool at Knole. Handling over the centuries has destroyed much of the original silver fringe

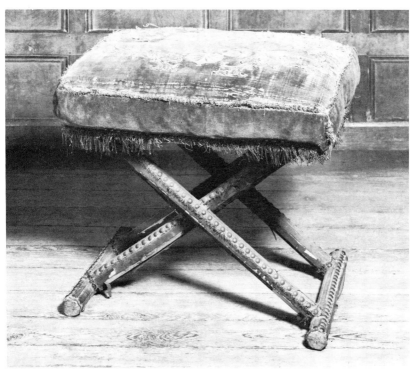

HANDLING

Fringes

Never touch the fringe when carrying furniture. Chairs and stools with fringes should always be carried by the legs by two people.

Carpets

Carpets can walk and ruck up against furniture which causes strain on the fibres and may result in the carpet getting torn. A carpet can be irreparably damaged by pulling at one end or corner when it is fully laid out. Its own weight and the friction on the floor can break the warp or weft. *Always* roll carpets and lift them into the new position even when only moving the carpet a few inches.

STORING

Textiles should be stored in the dark in a room which is both well ventilated and of even temperature. The relative humidity should be about 55 per cent and the temperature 5–15°C (40–60°F).

Store-rooms can be a breeding ground for pests so they must be kept clean. All stores should be examined once a year for signs of pests and mould.

Dust-free cupboard and drawer units are expensive. However, textiles can safely be stored in cupboards, open shelves or in large acid-free cardboard boxes. Line shelves and boxes with acid-free tissue paper. Open shelves should be curtained or dust-sheeted. Do not overfill boxes or cram shelves because textiles crush very easily.

List the textiles in store and when additions are made note the date so that the textile conservator can check the objects on the next visit.

Flat textiles

Small pieces can be laid flat, with each layer protected by acid-free tissue paper. Large textiles such as tapestries, carpets or banners should be rolled round a PVC tube or drain-pipe, or a cardboard tube 65–150mm (2½–6in) in diameter. The larger the dimensions of the object the greater the diameter of the tube must be. Rollers can sometimes be got from a local carpet shop. Cover all rollers with acid-free tissue paper before use.

Roll textiles firmly *right side out* in the direction of the warp threads. *Never* roll a textile right side in or it will get crushed. Take care that there are no folds or creases. Wrap each roll in a dust-sheet to exclude dust and light and, if it needs to be tied, use wide, white cotton tape. *Never* use rope or string, which can cut into the textile.

To roll a carpet

Never crush the carpet by folding it right side in or bundling it up. Roll carpets right side outside so that the pile is stretched rather than squeezed. This is easy with small rugs which can be turned over before rolling. It is rather more difficult when coping with a large carpet which should be rolled round a core of PVC or a cardboard roller (see above).

Clear the carpet of furniture. The more fragile the carpet the more people will be needed but do not start with less than three, and remove shoes before walking on the carpet. Stand on the carpet in a row facing one end of the carpet. Lift the edge and walk backwards for about three metres (three yards) so that the carpet is lying underside uppermost. Place the roller in position and roll up the end over the doubled area of the carpet so that the right side is outside. Stand on the carpet again facing the roller. Pick up the roller, and walk backwards for another three metres and roll this area of carpet; repeat until the whole carpet is on the roller.

Shaped textiles

Items that cannot be rolled should be laid out as flat as possible. Creases must be prevented from forming, so each fold should be padded out by a roll made up of acid-free tissue paper. Always re-fold in a different place, as holes will often appear along old crease lines.

DISPLAY

Lace

Lace may have to be washed and pinned out before being mounted. Consult an expert conservator.

Embroideries

Embroideries are sometimes framed and hung. The selection of acid-free mounts, the sealing of the glass and backing and the fitting of fillets to prevent the textile touching the glass should likewise be left to a conservator to arrange.

COSTUME

Cleaning and repairs

No cleaning or repairs should be done except under the direction of a textile conservator.

Display

Costume is best displayed on dummies in glass showcases where light and dust can be controlled. The room in which costume is displayed must be kept dry and aired throughout the year.

In winter, costume on open display should either be packed away in boxes or left on the dummy and covered with lightweight dust-sheets to exclude light and dust.

Dummies must be adapted to fit the particular costume. Do not use pins unless absolutely necessary. *Never* use steel dressmakers' pins which rust; use fine lace brass pins or stainless steel.

Storage

Hanging

Allow plenty of space between garments. A cotton cover can protect the costume from damage from buttons and hooks on adjoining garments. Cellulose acetate sheeting (Clarifoil) is a good alternative and has the advantage of being transparent. *Never* use polythene, as the static electricity which it stores attracts dust; polythene also inhibits ventilation, so that in some conditions condensation will form on it.

Pad coat-hangers with Terylene wadding or nylon stocking and then cover with calico or acid-free tissue paper. Do not use cotton wool to pad the hangers as it absorbs moisture.

If a dress has a waistline, sew tapes to the inside and loop these over the coat-hanger. The weight of the skirt will then be supported by the tape instead of by the shoulders of the garment. Puff out the sleeves with crumpled acid-free tissue paper.

Folding

Costumes can be folded and stored in large acid-free boxes. The garment should be laid out as flat as possible. Boxes with lids the same depth as the side of the box exclude dust and light best. Line the boxes with acid-free tissue paper and do not overfill as this squashes the lower layers and reduces the circulation of air. Soften each fold with a roll of acid-free tissue paper. Always re-fold a garment in a different place to prevent creases from forming. Often holes appear along an old crease.

Small garments such as blouses, underclothes, shoes, hats, gloves, etc., should be stored in boxes with plenty of acid-free tissue paper.

... a great deal of Paper is nowadays printed to be pasted upon Walls to serve instead of Hangings: and truly if all Parts of the Sheet be well and close pasted on, it is very pritty, clean and will last with tolerable Care a great while: but there are some other done by Rolls in long sheets of a thick Paper made for the Purpose whose sheets are pasted together to be so long as the Height of a Room – and they are managed like Woollen Hangings, and there is a great Variety, with curious Cuts [wood-cuts] which are Cheap, and if kept from Wet, very lasting.

John Houghton, F R S,
A Collection of Letters for the Improvement of Husban-
dry and Trade, 1689-1703

I saw a Chinese wallpaper when I was at Maigret's house with Mme de Forget. Maigret told us that we have nothing to equal their skill in producing fast colours, and he said that when he tried to make a sample of part of the pink background it turned a dreadful colour in a very short time ...

Extract from Eugene Delacroix's journal, 1847

67. Chinese wallpaper in the State Bedroom at Nostell Priory, supplied and hung by Thomas Chippendale in 1771

Although surviving sixteenth- and seventeenth-century wallpapers are rare and fragmentary, it is clear from contemporary records that wallpapers were both widely used and highly regarded.

The idiosyncratic production methods of the early manufacturers make it impossible to outline exact procedures for conservation. Expert advice should always be sought, as every case requires individual treatment. Problems may arise from the paper support, the ground and pigment layers, from adhesion between these components or between the paper and the wall surface. Similar difficulties exist with eighteenth- and nineteenth-century wall coverings and even modern papers.

If wallpapers are seen to be detached from the wall surface, the area should be investigated for the cause – this could be damp conditions, movement of the building, deterioration of the backing or even problems arising from previous layers. The wallpaper should not be re-attached without consulting an expert.

The paper-hanging makers

The success and ultimate prosperity of the English paper-hanging maker was due to several factors: the amount of technical knowledge already available to him, his ability to adapt to new forms of production to meet new fashions and his ability to produce convincing imitations of a variety of decorative hangings such as textiles, leather works and Chinese papers.

Although the 'superior' papers were usually put up by the maker, there is evidence to suggest that, from the early 1700s, do-it-yourself was acceptable. The detailed diagrams given in Diderot's *Encyclopédie* show that paper-hanging could be a very elaborate and complicated art indeed, and that the best work required the services of several expert operators, all of whom played a specially appointed part in the undertaking.

The early methods of hanging papers were varied, one of the commonest being described with deceptive simplicity by Robert Dunbar writing in 1734:

Please to observe the following Method of putting up the said Hangings in any Room viz:

First, Cut one Edge of each Piece or Breadth, even to the Work, then nail it with large Tacks to the Wall and paste the Edge of the next Breadth over the heads of the Tacks and so from one to another, till the Room be perfectly hung, observing to make ye Flowers join.

NB. Damp the Paper before you put it up, and begin next the window, and make stiff Paste of the best Flour and Water.

Gradually the papers themselves and the degree of finish expected of the hanging become finer. With the advent of roller-printed papers with accurate repeats, exact matching from piece to piece became possible, but it remained customary until relatively recent times to paste up sheets with an overlap. The edges of all papers required hand trimming and paper-hangers only adopted butted joints when accurate pre-trimming became widely available.

Until the late nineteenth century, the pastes were usually starch, the glues animal or fish based, and they were strong and water soluble. Modern pastes are derivatives of starch or polymethyl cellulose, and contain a fungicidal agent.

LEATHER AND 'WAX' CLOTH

Leather hangings

From early times leather was in common use for wall covering. The earliest decorated leather hangings were introduced by the Arabs who brought them from north Africa to Spain in the eleventh century. In the reign of the Emperor Charles V Spanish craftsmen in turn brought the art of leather painting and gilding to the Netherlands, whence it spread to England in the seventeenth century. English craftsmen under Dutch and Flemish influence also made hangings, screens and table covers, and were subsequently associated with the production of 'paper-hangings'.

Treatment is under review; in the meantime take relative-humidity readings in any room in which leather is hanging and *never* let sunlight fall directly on to the leather. *Never* attempt to clean leather hangings.

'Wax' cloth hangings

These hangings were tough, durable and almost impervious to damp conditions. Their production coincided with the vogue for chinoiserie effects and designs, and dimensions usually compared with contemporary paper-hangings.

Linen or canvas was stretched on to a wooden frame and given a ground of chalk/varnish/soot. This was smoothed with pumice, the design painted or printed on and a layer or layers of varnish added. Although the final varnish layer will give protection, the instability of the original ground must be respected and protected from adverse conditions of relative humidity.

CHINESE WALLPAPERS AND ENGLISH PAPERS IN THE CHINESE TASTE

It is generally accepted that Chinese papers first appeared in Europe about 1650. They were called India papers as they were transported in the ships of the Dutch, French and English East India Companies during their trading ventures with Canton. The impact of Chinese decorative art was felt in France from the 1650s, but English awareness came much later. John Evelyn, inspecting the Queen's collection of rare *objets d'art* in 1693, gives a matter-of-fact description of these 'divers China and India articles' which suggests that he was familiar with the vogue at this date.

68. One panel of a series of early-eighteenth-century wall hangings of embossed and gilded leather at Oxburgh Hall

Most of the Chinese papers were sold in sets of about twenty-five rolls, each twelve feet long. The absence of any kind of repeat, and the studied dissimilarity of detail between one length and another, gave them a unique quality which was greatly prized by those who possessed a room decorated and furnished in the oriental style. Each Chinese room should be regarded as an individual achievement. The sheets were normally hung from cornice to dado. Some meticulous paper-hangers carefully cut the painted decoration and embellished the panels with specially made matching borders.

The favourite motifs of the Chinese papers up to 1750 were flowering trees, shrubs and flowers with additions of birds, butterflies and small insects. The highest branches of the trees reached the extreme top edge of the sheet, and this section is frequently missing owing to the problems of fitting the sheet or the panel on to the existing wall space. Later examples specialized in landscape and figure motifs, the latter sometimes depicting Chinese life and occupations.

Chinese papers were essentially a luxury article (three to five guineas a roll in the eighteenth century) and special care was taken with their display. It is generally accepted that the Chinese style passed out of fashion during the latter half of the eighteenth century largely because of over-exaggerated designs.

The quality and design of the chinoiserie papers made by English artists varied greatly, from very fair reproductions of the flowering tree and shrub variety to the quaintest imitations of the landscape and figure types in which men and women in eighteenth-century garb are depicted wandering through improbable Far Eastern scenery, or taking their ease on seats of unmistakably English design. A surprisingly early English imitator was the stationer, James Minnikin, of St Martins le Grand, who advertised 'Japan' paper-hangings made on the premises for sale in 1680.

Structure

The rolls of panels were often formed of single sheets of paper, of approximately 51 × 76 cm (20 × 30 in), joined by a slight overlap of approximately 3 mm (⅛ in). This was backed with a long-fibred oriental paper of similar dimensions but with the seam falling in the centre of the decorated sheet, or sometimes even applied at right angles to the decorated sheet. The panels were often sized with alum before painting to prevent spreading of the pigments, which were bound with an animal-glue medium. The alum size may be responsible for the slight yellowing often visible in such papers and may also cause problems when the paper has been applied directly on to a plaster surface or an exterior wall. The panels were generally applied to a European or English lining paper, or, if professionally hung, to a canvas lining which was then stretched over wooden battens. The latter method is the most prevalent; it does allow the ventilation necessary to discourage mould growth, but presents problems of discoloration from contact with the wood or poor-quality canvas.

General care

Too much light causes irreversible fading and deterioration. Blinds should be kept down at all times and artificial light must be kept as low as possible (50 lux maximum).

Pieces of furniture should not be pushed up against wallpapers, particularly those stretched on battens.

Metal fixtures such as blind cleats or light switches should be isolated from the paper layer by an acid-free cartridge paper cut-out. (Metallic salts react with the pigments in adverse conditions of relative humidity and cause irreversible colour changes.)

The papers should not be allowed to come into contact with moisture or solvent fumes such as those from metal-cleaning agents, wood preservatives or fungicide agents. Tears, sags or loose areas should be reported to a conservator and *not* re-attached.

Do not dust the surface as such papers are very fragile, and subject to flaking and general deterioration. A paper conservator should be consulted before any treatment is undertaken.

FLOCK WALLPAPER

Although flocking on textiles was available much earlier, the first known examples of flocked paper suggest that this had become the usual medium by the end of the seventeenth century. The first types were coarse flock grounds built up in layers to resemble velvet; designs of figures and flowers were introduced with improved manufacturing techniques during the eighteenth century.

The technique involves passing paper, on which the design has been printed or stencilled in slow-drying adhesive, through the flock or powdered wool. The beauty and expense of these papers ensured careful treatment, with the consequent preservation of many fine examples.

General care

Do not attempt to clean or dust. Some flocks were made using powdered coloured silk instead of wool, and others have additional constitutents such as mica or metallic dusts to simulate gold and silver. These composites are particularly fragile and the adhesion of the various particles to the paper support may be weak.

He [the Rubber] is under the Direction of the Housekeeper to Dry rub the Floors in the House ... and assist upon the Ladders in Washing the wainscot and cornishes ...

Any fee given by any Person or Persons who come out of curiosity to see ye house shall be divided viz.

To the housekeeper 1/5

To the rubber 1/5

To the housemaids 3/5

From the servants' instructions at
Boughton House, Northamptonshire,
in the time of John, 2nd Duke of Montagu (*c.* 1730)

WALLS, WINDOWS AND CEILINGS

69. The Long Gallery at Sudbury. Intricate plasterwork ceilings of this type have to be cleaned from a lightweight tower scaffold

·❖ WALLS, WINDOWS AND CEILINGS ❖·

Step-ladders

Lightweight aluminium step-ladders suitable to the needs of the house are essential. It is a false economy not to replace existing wooden ladders, which are often heavy and unsteady. Cheap, badly designed equipment can be dangerous. Try out the step-ladder before buying it; some of the taller ones have back legs which bend and slip on polished floors.

The vulnerability of objects and decoration in a room should always be considered. Except when short and light, step-ladders should be carried by two people; one person alone should not attempt to shift the position of a long step-ladder, as it is easily unbalanced. The cost of conservation and decoration is too great to take the risk of damaging plasterwork, paintings or furniture.

Tower scaffolding

Houses with carved cornices, plasterwork, chandeliers, tapestries, large curtains and elaborate pelmets or picture frames need a lightweight aluminium tower scaffold, which is also useful when moving large paintings. This is an expensive piece of equipment and should be chosen with care.

DECORATIVE CARVED WOOD AND PLASTERWORK

Decorative carved mouldings and cornices should be vacuumed once a year. Care should be taken that dust does not fall on the paintings and tapestries beneath, and wall or ceiling paintings should not be touched. Care should be taken to move all small or vulnerable objects out of the way before starting work.

Depending on the size of the room use the Electrolux 350 E or Hoover Dustette. In very large rooms it is advisable to work from a tower scaffold.

Brush out finely carved mouldings with a hogshair fitch; for larger areas use a paper-hanger's brush. Fit the Hoover Dustette with the flexible hose and 'crevice head, protecting plasterwork from accidental knocks by binding a piece of foam rubber round the crevice head. By brushing out with one hand while holding the Dustette head in the other the dust is sucked up and does not float all over the room.

At the same time the opportunity should be taken to examine woodwork for woodworm and all decorative work for loose areas, cracks or rust stains. Any signs of these problems should be reported to an architect or conservator. Rust stains are evidence that the decoration has been put together with iron cramps or dowels, and when these rust they expand and cause the plasterwork to crack, just as with stone and marble sculpture.

Before attempting to wash paintwork, consider the overall effect of leaving high water marks which may make the wall look dirtier than before. Paintwork can be washed gently with warm water to which a little Synperonic N has been added. Rinse off and dry. Use three cloths and two buckets.

Obstinate marks, such as those left round door handles and on skirting boards after polishing, can sometimes be lifted by using a mixture of 50/50 white spirit and water to which a very little Fairy Liquid has been added (0.3 l, ¼ pint, of water to the same of white spirit and one teaspoon Fairy Liquid). First test the surface, as white spirit softens some paints. Apply the mixture with small swabs of cotton wool and use very sparingly. Rinse and dry well.

Do not use any commercial cleaning detergents or abrasive powders which can remove the surface of the paint or roughen it so that dirt will collect more easily.

Unpolished panelling

Dust over with a soft, dry duster or vacuum. Brush out carving with a hogshair fitch used in conjunction with the Hoover Dustette (see Decorative carved wood and plasterwork, p. 225).

Polished panelling

Treat in the same way as furniture (see Polished wood surfaces, p. 86).

Stained glass and leaded windows

The term 'stained glass' is applied to two main types of coloured glass, that made by adding pigment to the glass during manufacture and that produced by painting the surface of clear glass before firing.

Examine once a year for signs of weakness in the lead, which is shown by the window bowing out of its true vertical shape. If bowing or cracks in the glass are noticed these should be reported to a conservator.

Stained glass

This should *never* be washed because the paint is often loose on old glass, particularly heraldic glass, and this can very easily be dislodged and lost by washing. *Never* treat stained glass with UV-absorbent varnish or film.

Plain leaded glass

This can be wiped with a damp cloth, but do it very gently as some of the glass will be old and extremely fragile. Do not use any commercial detergent or window-cleaning product. The importance of the plain leaded glass should be established before it is treated with UV-absorbent varnish or film.

All other types of windows

Every house should have a check-list of windows treated with UV-absorbent varnish or film with the date of the last application. (See Appendix 1, p. 240.)

Windows treated with ultraviolet absorbent films or varnish

As there are many UV filters on the market, always check the manufacturer's cleaning instructions. Unless otherwise directed, wash with clean, clear water using a *clean* soft cloth. Dry gently without rubbing, using a soft cloth. Any particle of dust or grit can scratch the surface and damage the filter so the cloths must be kept scrupulously clean.

Do *not* touch the windows for thirty days after treatment with UV-absorbent varnish.

Do *not* clean the window in hot sunlight or if there is any likelihood of frost.

Do *not* use any detergent, cleaning agent or alcohol. (Methylated spirits is the solvent used to remove this varnish.)

Do *not* use brushes, chamois leather or paper towels.

Do *not* put any sticky tape or notices on the treated glass.

Untreated windows

Wash with clean water to which a little methylated spirits has been added. Use a soft, clean cloth. Dry and then polish the glass with chamois leather. Avoid proprietary cleaners which are expensive and dry out leaving white powder in the corners and along the edges. Also, many of these products contain silicone, which inhibits the adhesion of UV-absorbent varnish and makes it impossible to treat the window.

I sat down beside the fireplace and let my eyes wander over the miscellany of the room. There were many dusty objects lying around and heaped upon each other. It was like the lumber-room of Prince Prigio. Like him, I began to examine them. Each had its own significance as part of a place that breathed a story of its own. There are houses which have soul and spirit, inclined to joy or sorrow; there are places of dignity and grandeur. There are facades of brick and stone that hold images; there are little silent places where, in half-forgotten whispers in dusty corners, the stories of ages find voice.

Margaret Meade-Fetherstonhaugh,
Epilogue to *Uppark and its People*, 1964

MISCELLANEOUS

70. Model ships on display at Arlington Court

·✤ MISCELLANEOUS ✤·

The nap on the bed-cloth of a billiard table runs from the balk end to the spot end. On the cushions the direction of the nap varies according to the make of the table. The cloth is stretched tightly over the table when first fitted, but its natural characteristics allow it to stretch and in time it becomes slack. When this stage is reached, re-stretching by a skilled fitter is required.

Cleaning

Regular brushing and ironing with special billiard table equipment in the direction of the nap are essential to the maintenance of the table's efficiency.

1. Brush to remove all the dirt, using only the tip of the brush at the ends of the table.
2. Go over the table again with a duster wrapped round the brush.
3. Iron, using a clean warm iron; an iron that is too hot dries out the wool fibres making them brittle and the cloth becomes more susceptible to wear. Iron the bed-cloth only. *Never* iron the cushions.
4. Brush the cushions with the run of the nap.

DISPLAY CASES

Particularly fragile or brittle material may be displayed in rooms which are otherwise unsuitable by taking advantage of the relatively controlled conditions within a display case. The micro-climate of the case may be regulated by using recommended lining materials, such as cotton and/or good-quality acid-free paper, which will respond to varying degrees of temperature and relative humidity within the case and so steady the fluctuations towards an acceptable average. Care should be taken that cases are constructed of acid-free materials. Some cases made of wood have in the past caused much damage to exhibits put into them, because of the migration of acid from the wood.

The problems of lighting and ventilation should be considered by a specialist, as they are intimately related to the type and size of the case and also the nature of the material to be displayed.

Lighting

Ideally, lighting should be external to the case, in a top or side panel. This overcomes the problem of heat build-up (generated as a by-product of light) and enables maintenance to be carried out without disturbing the display.

Existing cases with interior lighting should have special low-temperature lights with an ultraviolet filter and a diffusing screen. Consult a lighting specialist.

At all times when the room is not in use the display case should be covered with a dense material such as velvet or felt so as to exclude all light.

Ventilation

Ventilation grilles should be positioned towards the top of the case to avoid foot-borne dust and dirt getting inside; if possible they should be placed at an angle to exclude settling dust. The grilles should be fitted with easily replaceable filters.

Relative humidity

Objects which require special conditions for their display – for example, enamels, waxes and illuminated parchment manuscripts – may involve the use of a desiccant or dehumidifying agent such as silica gel. These crystals respond to variations in relative humidity in a similar manner to case linings (see above) by stabilizing variations. The surface area of gel necessary depends on the volume of the case. The gel becomes saturated and contains a dye which changes colour to show when it should be replaced. Used silica gel has to be returned to the firm for reconditioning approximately once a year and a replacement supply should therefore also be kept. New cases for specially sensitive objects can be designed with trays for the gel (existing cases can be adapted following the advice of a conservator). A small hygro-meter (dial type) should be placed unobtrusively in these display cases and daily readings should be recorded where the objects are specially sensitive.

Rigidity

Suitably designed supports, covered with cotton or good-quality acid-free paper, should be provided for objects which could move or fall over if the display case were accidentally knocked. Pack the legs of the case if the floor is uneven.

Labels

Labels should be on good-quality acid-free paper or card placed near the object. Small stainless steel pins may be used to secure the label in position. *Never* attach a label to the object. *Never* use double- or single-sided Sellotape, Blu-tack or other adhesives.

Cleaning

No attempt should be made to clean or dust the objects once they have been arranged in a display case. If the display does appear dusty, or if there is any sign of deterioration in the exhibits, consult a conservator.

New cases

Never put items immediately into a new case or into one which has just been lined or relined. Leave the case open without objects in a well-ventilated room for a few weeks to allow resin and adhesive fumes to evaporate completely. Work on cases must therefore be carried out well ahead of the date on which a house is opened to the public.

Building and decorating work

When building or decorating is to be carried out in or near the room in which a case is displayed, remove the objects to another room which can be kept clean and dry. The objects should be transferred carefully, with clean hands, and placed on clean white blotting paper on a table or other flat surface. Cover them loosely with acid-free tissue paper and do not return the objects to the display case until at least two weeks after the redecoration work is completed and the paint fumes are entirely dispersed.

EPHEMERA

Posters, postcards, programmes, menu-cards, souvenirs, advertisements and a wide range of nineteenth- and twentieth-century paper items are involved in this category, the title of which admirably indicates their impermanence.

Owing to the transitory nature of the information they contain, these items were often made from poor-quality materials and were not usually treated with care. The high percentage of ground-wood fibres used in their manufacture is responsible for their rapid deterioration, which is accelerated by light, pollution and contact with other poor-quality items.

As they are often very brittle, ephemera should be handled as little as possible; do not attempt to unfold folded items – pick them up by the margins only. Unless on display, they should be stored in a Solander box, interleaved with acid-free tissue. The conservation of ephemera is highly specialized and a paper conservator should be consulted.

MODEL SHIPS

All model ships are extremely fragile. They must be handled as little as possible and should be displayed in glass cases.

They are made up from many types of organic materials such as bone, ivory, wood (especially pear wood) and textiles for the rigging and sails. All these materials are sensitive to variations in light levels, temperature and relative humidity. Above 50 lux colours will fade and the textile fibres deteriorate; direct sunlight or too strong electric light will increase the temperature inside a glass case. Temperature and relative-humidity levels are particularly important, as the delicate and finely cut parts of the model will dry out very quickly in adverse conditions, the deck planks will warp and overlap and marquetry will lift. If the relative humidity is too high and the case is damp, rigging will snap. Victorian rigging is painted to resemble tarring and is consequently more fragile than unpainted eighteenth-century rigging.

Ideal display conditions are a maximum light level of 50 lux and 55 per cent relative humidity with a temperature of 15°C (60°F).

Display

If the ships are kept in dust-free glass cases in the recommended conditions they will need little maintenance. As they are so fragile, cleaning of any sort should be left to an expert, who should inspect them every four or five years. Models were often varnished over layers of dirt, and decks may have been treated with oil and so have become dust traps. This needs specialist attention. *Never* cut off loose or broken rigging.

Transport

As the glass of a showcase is especially vulnerable to traffic vibrations, advice should be sought before any form of packing or transport is considered.

If an uncased ship has to travel it should be placed on a board which is longer than its entire length from bowsprit to stern and wider than the mainsail yard. Side pieces can then be fixed. The bowsprit and rigging are particularly fragile and should be well protected. Under no circumstances should packing material be allowed to come in contact with the model.

MUSICAL BOXES

Do not attempt to play a musical box unless it is known to be in safe working order. If in doubt consult an expert conservator of clocks who specializes in musical boxes.

If a box is played it is *essential* that the mechanism is only left stopped at the end of a tune. If the box is stopped or runs down in mid-tune the teeth of the comb are particularly vulnerable, especially if the box is moved.

In general the advice on positioning, care, maintenance and handling of musical boxes is exactly the same as that on clocks (see Chapter 4, pp. 59 ff.).

Positioning

It is especially important that musical boxes are not kept in hot conditions, such as in direct sunlight or near heating units, because with cylinder musical boxes the shellac cement slowly melts and sinks to the bottom of the cylinder.

Care and maintenance

As with clockwork, *never* attempt to clean, oil or touch the mechanism. Musical boxes are particularly vulnerable and if tampered with will readily self-destruct.

Handling

When moving a box, after making sure that it has been stopped at the end of a tune, a folded wedge of paper should be placed in the fan blades of the governor to ensure that the movement does not start during transit.

Also, where possible, the mainspring should be well run down by playing the box, as this will reduce still further the risk of an accident.

OBJETS D'ART

Coral

Treat in the same way as glass (see Glass, p. 97).

Enamels

Enamels are complex multi-layered works of art and should be handled with extreme care. Dust only occasionally with a ponyhair fitch and *never* use water, which could penetrate between the layers and set up corrosion, which would lead to surface loss.

Ivory

Ivory is an especially sensitive material: it is hygroscopic and has a strong directional grain. Keep out of direct sunlight and away from radiators. Never allow ivory to come into contact with water. Ivory should always be examined by an expert before cleaning is considered.

If ivory is to be stored it should be wrapped in acid-free tissue paper. *Never* use cotton wool, soft paper or cloth as these materials retain moisture, which will migrate into the ivory. Coloured paper or coloured cloth must also be avoided as moisture will transfer the dye to the ivory.

Jade

Treat in the same way as glass (see Glass, p. 97).

A housemaid's duty is to keep the housemaid's cupboard in order, and to be dressed by four or half-past four in the afternoon ...

From *The Servants Practical Guide*,
by the author of *Manners and Tone of Good Society*,
1880

APPENDICES

71. Double blinds in the Turner Room at Petworth

METHODS OF PROTECTION AGAINST LIGHT

As it is often impossible in a house to cut down the levels of light to museum recommended levels, it is essential to cut down the time the object is exposed to light by using shutters, sun-blinds and sun-curtains.

SHUTTERS

Where shutters exist they should be put into working order and used.

Since the exclusion of light prolongs the life of the object, shutters in National Trust houses are closed as soon as visitors leave and left shut until the house is opened up again. In summer the use of shutters can exclude six to eight hours of daylight.

As a temporary expedient, where sun-blinds have not yet been fitted, a shutter can sometimes be half-closed to prevent shafts of sunlight striking objects in the room.

During the winter months, when a house is closed, as much light as possible should be excluded, although adequate ventilation must be maintained.

SUN-BLINDS

As light levels have to be kept down, it is recommended that plain cream or buff holland blinds are fitted. These transmit a sunny sort of light even on a grey day. White blinds are not only less effective in cutting down the amount of light, but make even a sunny day seem rather cold.

When shutters are opened in the mornings, the sun-blinds should be pulled right down and left down, being raised only when the room is being cleaned, after which they should be lowered again. Where there are no shutters, sun-blinds should be pulled right down when the house closes in the evening and left down until the house opens, except, of course, during cleaning.

Sun-blinds in houses open to the public should not be raised in any room until the first visitors can be heard approaching; in large houses this can be as much as an hour after opening time.

A room in which there are delicate textiles, such as the hangings of a state bed, must be kept darker than, say, a dining-room. The human eye adapts to different light levels and so is a poor judge of light. This can be helpful in protecting the objects, since, provided that the reduction in light is not too dramatic, visitors can come from bright sunlight into a house with much reduced light levels with no loss of enjoyment.

The amount that the sun-blinds are raised cannot be left entirely to common sense. Light levels should be constantly checked with a light meter.

When a meter is used, it should face the source of light because it is the amount falling on the object that should be measured, not the light reflected from it (see Appendix 2, p. 245).

Direct sunlight should always be excluded – beware of the day that can start cloudy and become sunny. The height of the blinds should be adapted throughout the day to suit changing light conditions. The tops of windows with fanlights or gothic arches can be obscured by fitting into them a shaped piece of blind material. This can either be stretched over a frame which fits the window, or it can be fixed around the window frame with Velcro.

In very special cases, such as the Turner Room at Petworth, two blinds can be fitted. The normal cream holland blind nearer the window is kept permanently down, even when visitors are in the room, and a second dark green or blue blind, fitted on the room side of the cream blind, is raised by the room steward when there are visitors in the house, but kept down whenever the room is empty for long periods.

If an alarm system is to be fitted before sun-blinds or sun-curtains are in position, the security company should be warned. On a windy night, draughts coming through the closed window may move the blind or curtain. The type of alarm fitted should not be so sensitive as to be set off by this movement.

See also Selecting and fitting sun-blinds, opposite.

SUN-CURTAINS

In some cases, as for instance with the huge mullion windows at Hardwick, blinds are inappropriate and it may be possible to fit sun-curtains instead. The disadvantage of these is that they obscure the view from the window and tend to be claustrophobic. The advantage of sun-blinds is that they can be pulled down so that they block out the sky, while allowing the view below the skyline to be enjoyed.

There is a wide choice of sun-curtain material. The thicker and denser the material the more light it obscures. When making and hanging sun-curtains it is essential that the curtains overlap in the centre and come right to the window-frame edge, otherwise great shafts of light come into the room. The fullness of the curtain also lowers the light level.

TREATMENT OF WINDOWS WITH ULTRAVIOLET (UV) FILTERS

While the glass of all windows should ideally be treated with UV-absorbent varnish or film, certain rooms, in which there are exhibits specially sensitive to light, *must* be protected in this way. The manufacturer treats the glass and will provide special cleaning instructions. There is much more ultraviolet in daylight than in the light from fluorescent tubes.

Details of windows treated and dates should be kept at the house so that deterioration of the UV filter can be monitored and the cause of any damage determined.

UV-absorbent varnish

This has to be applied by a specialist who cleans the window and then treats it by running the varnish over the glass so that it forms a continuous coating. This work has to be carried out in the summer months as the varnish must dry overnight. The treatment is not recommended for windows which have a history of condensation because the water gets under the varnish at the edge of the pane and lifts it off, especially during freezing weather. The varnish can easily be damaged by abrasion and chemicals when cleaning the windows (see Windows, p. 226).

UV-absorbent film

These films have recently come on the market, a spin-off from space travel and from the need to prevent flying glass in bomb attacks. There are many varieties on the market but some are not as effective as they claim to be.

Film comes in sheets that have to be cut to the required window size.

UV-ABSORBENT JACKETS FOR FLUORESCENT TUBES

Ultraviolet radiation from unshielded fluorescent tubes causes damage so never install a fluorescent tube without fitting a UV-absorbent jacket. Fluorescent tubes are being manufactured to filter UV rays but are, as yet, more expensive and replacements may be difficult to get.

SELECTING AND FITTING SUN-BLINDS

It is unwise to accept the lowest estimate for fitting sun-blinds without first checking exactly what you are being offered. Blinds are expensive and if they jam or do not run smoothly they will not be used. The expense of a blind is divided fairly evenly in three: the cost of the roller, the cost of the material, and the labour for making up and fixing. Good-quality blinds should last many years without renewal.

Rollers

Selecting a roller suitable for the job is essential to the long life and smooth functioning of the blind.

Spring roller

To raise the blind, it must be pulled down slightly by the centre cord in order to release the check action on the end of the roller.

Seamed metal barrel rollers should be selected. Diameter varies according to drop from 4 to 6.5 cm (1½ to 2½ in). The larger the diameter of the roller the stronger the spring which can be fitted. *Never* fit cheap mass-produced aluminium rollers, which are not adequate either for a large drop or for constant use.

Cap-and-rack roller

Cap-and-rack rollers are inclined to leave a gap down the side of the window, letting in a streak of light.

This type of roller has a brass ratchet at one end and requires both hands to operate the blind. One hand controls the blind by the centre cord, while the other pulls the cord at one end of the roller about half an inch to release the blind. *Never* release the ratchet at the side without controlling the movement of the blind by the centre cord or the blind will zip up at terrific speed and wind the centre cord round and round the roller.

Old cap-and-rack rollers are often found stacked away somewhere in a house, usually with broken blinds attached. These rollers, with their brass ratchets, are well worth recovering for re-use. A lot of money can be saved in this way.

Flange-end roller

This type has no spring and the blind is constantly dropping unless secured by its cord on a K-cleat. It can be virtually any size. It is also useful when access to the blind is difficult as the cleat can be some distance from the blind.

Self-acting spring roller

For a glass roof, either sloping or flat, self-acting seamed metal spring rollers should be used. These have no check action but are always under tension. The blind is prevented from closing by a cord anchored on a K-cleat.

Any blind which does not hang vertically must be on a self-acting spring roller. Guide lines are fitted so that the blind travels in the direction of the glass instead of dropping vertically.

Material (or drop)

All blinds used to be made of window holland, a glazed linen which is now unobtainable. The best substitute is a synthetically treated cotton which is virtually indistinguishable from holland.

The drop should have tabling or side-hems and it is important that the stitching is zig-zag or cross stitch; a straight running stitch can buckle the edge. It is sometimes said that side-hems are not necessary on blinds made of the synthetically treated cotton because the material is less likely to fray. However, blinds traditionally had side-hems and on important windows they look rather mean without them.

The drop normally falls from the roller on the side nearer the window. Where fittings and handles would bruise and distort the blind, the drop can fall on the room side of the roller, which gives an extra two inches or so clearance.

The bottom edge of the blind should be fitted with a strong, pear-shaped stick, which should be stitched into its own pocket in the hem. It is to this stick that the knot holder is attached; many of the sticks now fitted are too thin and snap easily.

The knot holder, fixed through the bottom edge of the blind on to the stick, should be fitted on the side nearer the window, out of sight.

The cord from the knot holder should be in cotton or flax, *not* nylon. It is fitted with a wooden acorn (with a rubber band to prevent tapping), or a tassel, or a Turk's head. A tassel has a knot of 'silk' and fringe. A Turk's head has a bulbous 'silk' knot and no fringe. The cord should not have plastic fittings.

72. Examples of the wooden acorn that is traditionally attached to blind cords

It is never worth renewing the drop on existing cheap aluminium rollers, but it is well worth while renewing the material on the recommended types of seamed metal rollers.

Any existing blinds that are in constant need of attention should be renewed. However, a programme of work should be drawn up, as a fitter can measure or fit about ten or twelve blinds in a day and the manufacturer will charge a day's time whether one or a dozen blinds are measured or fitted. The fine adjustment of a blind is of great importance and so it should be fitted by a craftsman.

SPECIAL EQUIPMENT AND PROTECTION

The light levels recommended by museums are:

50 lux

Textiles (costumes, rugs, tapestries, curtains, etc)
Water-colours, prints, drawings, letters and documents
Photographs
Marquetry furniture
Miniatures
Natural-history specimens

200 lux

Oil paintings

Using light meters

The sensor of the light meter should always face the light and must not be obscured by a hand or shadows of bodies, etc. Remember that it is the amount of light falling on the object which should be read, not the light reflected from it. The meter should be held facing the light source and parallel to the object without touching it. The light level is measured in lux units.

Photometer S511

This instrument consists of a scale and a round light sensor over which can be fitted two black caps marked 2500 and 5000.
Without a cap, read the lower set of figures, 1-500
With 2500 cap, read the upper set of figures, 1-2500
With 5000 cap, read the lower set of figures, 1-5000

AVO LM4

This instrument consists of a scale and a square light sensor with a black switch. When switched to 500 read the top set of figures, 1-500; when switched to 2000 read the lower set of figures, 1-2000.

Further information

For further information consult: Gary Thomson, *The Museum Environment*, Butterworth, 1978.

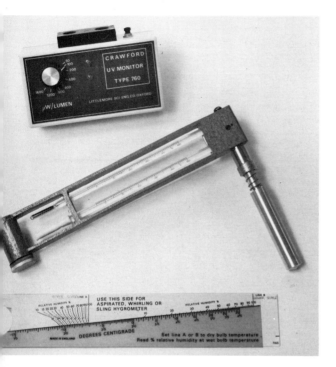

73 and 74. An ultraviolet monitor and a whirling hygrometer; and (right) a light meter

POCKET WHIRLING HYGROMETERS

Hygrometers are used to measure relative humidity.

Before use

1. Buy distilled water (from any chemist), an eye-dropper bottle (or equivalent) and a magnifying glass.
2. Cut the sleeve just below the wet bulb (making sure that the bulb is covered by the sleeve).
3. Store spare length of tubular wick (sleeve) in the reservoir tank (dry).

Using distilled water keeps the sleeve free of salts and other deposits. As the instrument is only going to be used once a week, it is not recommended that the reservoir tank is used as it would have to be emptied after use. It is also easier to keep the sleeve on a wet bulb clean if the wick is used in short lengths. Using the magnifying glass speeds up readings and helps prevent breathing on the bulbs.

246

Use

1. Push the adjustable ring on the handle into position so that the joint is firmly held.
2. While both bulbs are dry, it is important that the two thermometers should agree in their reading to within 0.2 °C.
3. Drop distilled water on the sleeve covering the wet bulb and allow time for it to soak in. (See that drops of water do not fall on the dry bulb, which must be dry – or dried – before the reading is taken.)
4. Whirl the hygrometer at arm's length for about half a minute.
5. Read the temperature of the wet bulb to a quarter of a degree.
6. Repeat the whirling and reading the wet bulb until three successive readings agree.
7. Record readings of wet bulb and dry bulb, taking care to keep hands away from the thermometers and not to breathe on the bulbs. Note the wet bulb first as it is less stable than the dry bulb.
8. Add drops of distilled water on the sleeve of the wet bulb before moving on to the next room to allow time for it to soak in. (It is essential that the wet bulb sleeve remains fully moistened throughout the operation.)

Directions for working out the relative humidity are given with every instrument.

DRUGGETS

Recommended druggets

The International Wool Secretariat carried out tests over two years at the Treasurer's House, York, and at Erddig in north Wales to determine the best type of drugget. This research has led to the following conclusions:
1. Druggets protect a carpet from dirt and wear by absorbing and dissipating impact. The thicker the drugget, the better the protection.
2. They should be used especially in areas through which visitors are channelled or at any point where there is a turn in the route.
3. The druggets recommended are:
   (a) *Wilton* This lets through least dirt and its thickness gives the best protection from impact. It should be used on the longer-pile carpets.
   (b) *Hairfelt or Feltlux* This came second to the Wilton and is recommended for short-pile carpets.
4. *Never* use plastic druggets because they can cause permanent structural damage to the carpet and may encourage mildew attack through condensation.

Practical points

1. Underfelt beneath a carpet is essential. Wear marks showed on a trial carpet without underfelt within six weeks. Good contract-quality hair-

felt mixed underlay took up all the unevenness of the floor leaving a smooth surface for the carpet. Rubber underlays merely followed the contours of the floor.

2. The druggets should:
   (a) be wide enough to enable the stanchions of the ropes to stand on the drugget;
   (b) cover all edges and ends of the carpet, which are very vulnerable areas – this is particularly important in window embrasures;
   (c) be laid with as few joins as possible, because any uneven line or roughness will cause wear. Some modern joining methods use adhesive tape which gives a smooth finish but the adhesive can leach out, marking the carpet.

3. All druggets should be taken up each winter, so that the carpets can be well vacuumed and the pile restored.

Fixing of druggets

1. If possible druggets should not be nailed through a carpet.
2. Short straight lengths are less likely to move. Rugstop, a special Terylene wadding, has proved effective in stopping movement.
3. As druggets should be lifted each winter, the fixing must be simple and not damage the floor. Recommended methods are:
   (a) a heavy metal bar sewn into a pocket at each end (suitable for felt druggets);
   (b) large-headed brass carpet pins and sockets fixed at approximately 15 cm (6 in) intervals;
   (c) a bar of wood (see fig. 17) – this is better than the more easily available narrow metal bars.

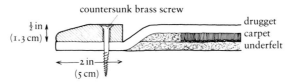

Fig. 24. Wooden bar used to fix drugget. It is held at 15 cm (6 in) intervals by brass screws in brass sockets. The carpet should not go under the bar; underfelt should be used to fill any space between the carpet and the bar

THE HOUSEMAID'S CUPBOARD

A housemaid's cupboard is essential for equipment and materials in constant use. It should be well lit, with adequate shelving space for materials, dusters, polish, etc., and an area for hanging mops and brushes. In a really large house there should be one of these cupboards on each floor.

Electrical equipment

Each house should decide on the type and quantity of equipment needed for the number of cleaning staff. The following electrical equipment has proved to be the most useful.

Vacuum cleaners

Small   *Hoover Dustette* S1122 with attachments S1914
Medium   *Electrolux 350 E*
Industrial   *Electrolux UZ 925*, complete with attachments
             Nilfisk GS 80, machine, trolley and 300 mm floor attachment. Extra attachments: 400 mm carpet head (114762), crevice tool (815304), and crevice brush (115305). If there is a lot of modern carpet and drugget the power brush (15010252) and reducer (815037) may also be necessary.
             Numatic Caretaker NV 250, complete with attachments

Polishers

Domestic   *Electrolux B 23*
Industrial   *Columbus Dixon UB 826*

Scrubbing machines

Columbus Dixon UB 826

Wet suction machines

Columbus Dixon UZ 866

The larger pieces of equipment are heavy and so difficult to move from floor to floor. They should therefore be stored near the largest area that has to be cleaned.

If the rooms open to the public cover several floors it is better to duplicate the smaller pieces of equipment such as the Dustette and Electro-lux 350 E so that each floor has its own. Much time can be lost searching for the equipment and carrying it to the area where it is needed.

Brushes

Brushes must be kept for the job specified. *Never* use one brush for different purposes. For example, *never* use a Silver Dip brush for dusting bronze; *never* use a furniture-polish brush on gilding. As it is important to distinguish the purpose of a particular brush, mark the handle of the brush so that it is readily recognizable.

To prevent metal ferrules scratching surfaces, isolate them by wrapping insulating tape round the top of the metal ferrule.

Brushes must be washed periodically. If waxy, first rinse in white spirit, then wash thoroughly with soap and water, rinse well under running water and allow to dry naturally (without heat) before storing.

See also Appendix 4, p. 253.

Dust-sheets and winter covers

Dust-sheets must be lightweight, closely woven cotton and should be washed every year. This is particularly important if there have been builders in the house.

When the house is 'put to bed', furniture can be covered with loose cotton dust-covers. These covers or sheets should be marked with their position in the room and stored in that room when not in use. All case covers must be made with french seams as loose threads can stick to upholstery or catch and pull off pieces of veneer and metal decorations.

Care of chamois leather

Never use any detergents (powder or liquid) on chamois leather. They will react with and destroy the natural oils in the skin. Fairy soap is acceptable but Fairy Liquid is a detergent. Wash chamois leather in warm soapy water; rinse out well in clean water; never wring out excess water but squeeze gently and shake out flat; allow to dry slowly away from direct heat and never in sunlight as heat and sunshine will also destroy the natural oils in the skin. Rub together to bring back the softness of the leather.

Synperonic N

This is a neutral (non-ionic) detergent which acts as a wetting agent, breaking the surface tension of the water and enabling it to penetrate more easily. It

75 and 76. The Linen Room and (below) the Housemaids' Room, in Queen Mary's Dolls' House

comes in a highly concentrated form and must be used very sparingly: one teaspoon to one tablespoon to a gallon of water, depending on the type and amount of dirt. It froths very easily. If too much is used it is extremely difficult to rinse off. Pure Synperonic N is colourless and practically odourless.

77. A modern housekeeper's room at Dunham Massey

APPENDIX 4

SUPPLIERS OF EQUIPMENT
AND MATERIALS

While believing the information given in the Manual to be correct at the time of going to press, the National Trust can take no responsibility for any shortcomings in service by the suppliers listed below or any deficiencies in their products.

Note. Address of supplies given in *italic* type will be found in Appendix 5, pp. 258 ff.

Acid-free envelopes, folders
Made to order, any size
   C. A. Coutts Ltd

Acid-free mounting card and board
   Conservation Resources UK Ltd
   Lawrence & Aitken
   Falkiner Fine Papers Ltd (single sheets)

Acid-free paper – cartridge paper
   Lawrence & Aitken
   Falkiner Fine Papers Ltd (single sheets)

Acid-free tissue paper
   Spicer Cowan Ltd (ream packs – 500 sheets approx.)
   Small quantities from stationers – but make sure that it is acid-free

Aluminium step-ladders (lightweight)
   Local ironmonger

Anti-static liquid spray for Perspex
   Amari Plastics Ltd

Artist's portfolio
   A specialist art shop

Aubo Bronze picture wire
   J. Shiner & Son Ltd

Balsa wood
   Model aeroplane shop

Beeswax, pure (not bleached)
   W. S. Jenkins & Co. Ltd

Billiard-table maintenance
Electric iron; brush
   Raper & Sons Ltd

Black lead (see Zebrite)

Boxes
Low acid and specialist boxes
   C. A. Coutts & Co. Ltd
   Conservation Resources (UK) Ltd

Solander boxes
Invented by a Dr Solander for storing prints and drawings at the British Museum.
Made to order, any size
   G. Ryder & Co.

Wire-stitched record boxes
   C. A. Coutts Limited

Brass framing plates
To be used instead of nails; no. 1, 2, 3, 4, with round-headed $\frac{3}{8}$ in/$\frac{1}{2}$ in brass screws
   J. Shiner & Sons Ltd

Brushes
Banister brush
Black lead brush
Furniture (bristle shoe brush, curved end)
Hogshair fitch (firm but soft)
Plate brush (curved, 4-row)·
Plate brush (straight, 6-row)
Ponyhair fitch (very soft)
Radiator brush
   Available by post from The National Trust (Enterprises) Ltd, Western Way, Melksham, Wiltshire

Paint brush ($\frac{1}{2}$ in)
Wallpaper-hanger's brush
   Local ironmonger or DIY shop

Bubble wrap (polythene air-cap)
   Costerwise Ltd (bulk order)
   Spicer Cowan Ltd ('Aircap')
   Transatlantic Plastics (small order)

Calico
   Local store
   MacCulloch & Wallis
   H. Wolfin & Son Ltd
   Quarry Bank Mill Trust Ltd

Cardboard rollers (see also PVC pipes)
   Local carpet or dress-fabric shops

Carpet paper
Local carpet shop

Carpet pins and sockets (brass)
Size 1½ and 2 in
James Smith & Son (Redditch) Ltd

Cellulose acetate sheeting (Clarifoil)
Sheet sizes 24 × 56 in (61 × 142 cm) in various
gauges
A. Warne & Co. Ltd

Chamois leathers
Wilson (Wearwell) Ltd

**Coconut matting (treble plain quality) and
coir fibre mats**
Local manufacturers
Norfolk Industries for the Blind

Cotton glacie picture cord
J. Shiner & Son Ltd

Cotton gloves (without cuffs)
Wilsons (Wearwell) Ltd

Cotton wool
Local chemist

Cuprinol Woodworm Killer Low Odour
Local ironmonger
Cuprinol Ltd

Curtain rings and hooks
W. E. Hudson

Cuticle-sticks – round, wooden
Local chemist

Detergent – neutral, non-ionic
Synperonic N
Frank W. Joel

Discs (for furniture)
3-ply or hardboard
Local carpenter

Distilled water
Local chemist; NOT from a garage

Doormat (see Coconut matting)

Dusters (all varieties)
Local supplier
Wilsons (Wearwell) Ltd

Dust-sheets
Wilsons (Wearwell) Ltd
Ulster Weaving Co. (made to order)

Electrolux
350 Electronic Domestic Vacuum Cleaner
UZ930 Light Industrial Vacuum Cleaner
B23 Floor Polisher
Electrolux Limited

Felt
Local haberdasher or carpet shop

Feltlux
Local carpet shop
Bury & Masco Industries Ltd

Filtration fabric (see Nylon screening)

Fly swat (plastic)
Local ironmonger

Foam rubber sheeting (¼–½ in)
Local supplier

Hide food (Connolly's)
Local saddler
Connolly Bros.

Hoover Dustette S1122
Attachments S1914
Hoover Ltd

Hygrometers
Whirling
Russell Scientific Instruments Ltd
Dial
Casella London Ltd

Ladders (see Aluminium ladders)

Light meters
Photometer S511
Megatron Ltd
Avo LM4
Thorn EMI Instruments Ltd

Long Term Silver Cloth
Local ironmonger
*J. Goddard & Co. Ltd (see Johnson Wax
Ltd)*

Long Term Silver Foam
Local ironmonger
*J. Goddard & Co. Ltd (see Johnson Wax
Ltd)*

Mafu
Local ironmonger

Metal hangers for ceramic plates
Department store

Methylated spirits (inflammable)
Local chemist or ironmonger

Mops
Local ironmonger

Mothballs
Local chemist or ironmonger

Muslin, butter
MacCulloch & Wallis

Mutton cloth
Wilsons (Wearwell) Ltd

Mystox LPL 100%
Mothproofing fluid based on pentachloro-phenyl laurate used as a 5% solution in white spirit
Picreator Enterprises Ltd

Naptha flakes
Local chemist

Nilfisk GS 80
Industrial vacuum, machine-trolley and 300 mm floor attachment
Extra attachments: 114762 400 mm carpet
              nozzle
              815304 crevice tool
              115305 crevice brush
With a lot of modern carpets and druggets the following may also be necessary:
              15010252 power brush
              815037 reducer
Nilfisk Ltd

Numatic
Caretaker NV 250 industrial vacuum
Numatic International

Nylon line
Local fishing-tackle shop

Nylon net
20–20 denier No. 2014 132 cm wide
40–20 denier No. 1595 132 cm wide
Natural colour
Black Brothers and Boden

Nylon screening
Picreator Enterprises Ltd

Paint
International Matt Black
Manders Black Ebony Finish M.757
   Local paint shop
   Manders Paints Ltd

Paradichlorobenzene
Local chemist

Picture chain, cord and wire
   J. Shiner & Sons Ltd

Picture hooks
   J. Shiner & Sons Ltd

Picture rail
$\frac{3}{4}$ in gas pipe
Local builders' merchant

Picture rail hooks and fittings
   J. Shiner & Sons Ltd

Pins
Stainless steel and 1 in lace brass
Local haberdasher
   MacCulloch & Wallis Ltd

Plastic injector bottle
Rentokil produces a small plastic bottle with a special applicator for injecting insecticide fluid.
   Local ironmonger

Plastic bags (self-sealing)
   Transatlantic Plastics

Plastic slippers
   HPC Group

Plastic tubing
Local chemist

Polish
1. Floor
   Johnson's Traffic Wax (liquid or paste)
   Steadfast (liquid, quick drying)
      Johnson Wax Ltd
      Small quantity – local ironmonger
2. Furniture wax
   National Trust Furniture Wax
      sold in National Trust shops
3. Brass, copper (see Solvol Autosol)

4. Grates, black lead (see Zebrite)
5. Silver (see Silver Dip, Long Term Silver Cloth and Long Term Silver Foam)
6. Steel (see Solvol Autosol)

Polisher, electric
Small
Electrolux (B23)
Industrial
Columbus Dixon (UB826)

Polyester transparent envelopes (photographs)
Secol Ltd

Polystyrene blocks
Arrowtip Ltd

Polystyrene pellets or chips
Costerwise Ltd (bulk orders)
Arrowtip Ltd (by the bag)

PVC pipes (see also Cardboard rollers)
Drainpipes
Local builders' merchants

Renaissance Wax
Picreator Enterprises Ltd

Rollers (see Cardboard rollers or Plastic pipes)

Rope (worsted), hooks and eyes
Beardmore & Co. Ltd (1 in, 1¼ in, 1½ in)
J. Wippell & Co. Ltd

Rugstop
Local carpet shop
A. S. Parker & Co. Ltd

Rush matting
Waveney Apple Growers

Sable brush
An art shop

Scaffold tower (lightweight)
Yellow Pages
Martin-Thomas Ltd – Hi-Way
John Rusling Ltd – Rib-grip

Scrubbing machine
Columbus Dixon – UB826

Shaving brush
Local chemist

Silica gel
Self-indicating (coarse)
Local builders' merchant or chemist

Silver Dip – Goddard's
Solution for removing tarnish from silver
Local ironmonger
J. Goddard & Co. Ltd (see *Johnson W Ltd*)

Solvol Autosol
Fine paste used for cleaning and polishing steel, brass and copper
Local car accessory firm
Solvolene Lubricants Ltd

Stainless steel brackets
Local builders' merchant

Stanchions
Roblin & Sons
Beardmore & Co. Ltd
J. Wippell & Co. Ltd

Steel wool – fine grades 000 and 0000
W. S. Jenkins

Stiletto heel guards
Aztec Tooling & Moulding Co.

Stoddarts Solvent (see white spirit)

Sun-blinds
Local specialist blind manufacturer
Tidmarsh & Sons

Sun-curtains
Made from material of natural and/or man-made fibre.
A department store or specialist fabric shop

Synperonic N (see Detergents)

Syringe for treating woodworm
Frank Joel (Cat. No. LS8)

Tape – broad white
Local haberdasher

Terylene wadding
Local haberdasher

Treasurers' filing tags
Local stationer

Turpentine (oil of pure – inflammable and poisonous)
Supplied in various degrees of purity. Do NOT use turps substitute.
  Local ironmongers

UV-absorbent sleeves for fluorescent tubes
122 cm (4 ft) lengths
  Bonwyke Ltd
  The Morden Company (minimum order 12)

UV-absorbent treatment of window glass
Film
  Bonwyke Ltd (FSW 200 Clear)
  Solar X (UK) Ltd (Solar X PVI 200)
Varnish (applied by *John Chamberlain*)
  The Morden Company (Anti-sol)

UV meter
Elsec Crawford UV Monitor Type 760
  Littlemore Scientific Engineering Co.

Underfelt
Good contract quality. Hair/jute blend: Gaskell Defender + or 472
  Local carpet dealer
  Gaskell & Co.

Vacuums
Lightweight, see Hoover Dustette
Medium, see Electrolux 350 Electronic
Industrial, see Electrolux UZ 925
        Nilfisk GS 80
        Numatic Caretaker NV 250

Vapona
  Local hardware store

Velcro
Nylon strip 'touch and close' fastener
  All widths from *Velcro Ltd*
  Narrow widths from local haberdasher

Watering can
  Local ironmonger or garden shop

Webbing (heavy duty)
When handling furniture, to hold doors and drawers closed.
  Local haberdashers
  Upholsterers

Wet suction machine
  Columbus Dixon Ltd (UZ 866)

Weedkiller bar (for watering rush matting)
  Local ironmonger or garden shop

White blotting paper
  Local stationer
  Wiggins Teape (Fords Gold Medal)

White spirit (inflammable)
Supplied in various degrees of quality
  Local ironmonger

Wilton carpet
  Local carpet shop

Wire scraping mats
  Weetman & Co.

Wire trays (plastic coated)
Sold for correspondence, vegetables and freezers
  Local stationers or ironmongers

Zebrite (black lead, in tubes)
  Local ironmonger

SUPPLIERS' ADDRESSES

Amari Plastics Limited
Amari House
52 High Street
Kingston-upon-Thames
Surrey KT1 1HN
01-549 6122

Arrowtip Ltd
Arrowtip House
31–35 Stannary Street
London SE11 4AA
01-735 8848

Aztec Tooling and Moulding Co.
3–7 Raglan Street
Worcester WR3 8AY
0905 611863

J. D. Beardmore & Co. Ltd
3–5 Percy Street
London W1P 0FJ
01-637 7041

Black Brothers & Boden
53 Stoney Street
Nottingham NG1 1NA
0602 505772

Bonwyke Ltd
41 Redlands Lane
Fareham
Hampshire PO14 1HL
0329 289621

Bury, Cooper, Whitehead Ltd
Hudcar Lane
Bury
Lancashire BL9 6HD
061-764 2262

Casella London Ltd
Regent House
Britannia Walk
London N1 7ND
01-253 8581

John Chamberlain
88 Wensley Road
Woodthorpe
Nottingham
0602 269424

Columbus Dixon Ltd
Oakley Road
Luton
Bedfordshire LU4 9QQ
0582 580120

Connolly Bros. (Curriers) Ltd
Wandle Bank
South Road
Wimbledon
London SW19 1DW
01-542 5251

Conservation Resources (UK) Ltd
Unit 1
Littleworth Industrial Estate
Wheatley
Oxfordshire OX9 1TZ
086 772244

Costerwise Ltd
16 Rabbit Row
London W8 4DX
01-221 0666

C. A. Coutts Ltd
Violet Road
London E3 3QL
01-515 6171

Cuprinol Ltd
Adderwell
Frome
Somerset BA11 1NL
0373 65151

Electrolux Ltd
Oakley Road
Luton
Bedfordshire LU4 9QQ
0582 573255

Falkiner Fine Papers Ltd
117 Long Acre
Covent Garden
London WC2E 9PA
01-379 6245

Gaskell & Co. (Bacup) Ltd
PO Box 10
Lee Mill
Bacup
Lancashire OL13 0DJ
0706 874381

Hoover plc
Perivale
Greenford
Middlesex UB6 8DX
01-997 3311

HPC Group
30 Commerce Road
Brentford
Middlesex TW8 8LE
01-568 7973

W. A. Hudson
115–125 Curtain Road
London EC2A 3QS
01-739 3211

W. S. Jenkins & Co. Ltd
Jeco Works
Tariff Road
Tottenham
London N17 0EN
01-808 2336/7

Frank W. Joel
Oldmeadow Road
Hardwick Industrial Estate
Kings Lynn
Norfolk PE30 4HH
0553 60851

Johnson Wax Ltd (Goddard, same address)
Frimley Green
Camberley
Surrey GU16 5AJ
0276 63456; service centre 0276 24078 (24 hours)

Lawrence & Aitken
Albion Works
Kimberley Road
London NW6 7SL
01-624 8135

Littlemore Scientific Engineering Co.
Railway Lane
Littlemore
Oxford OX4 4PZ
0865 778402

Macculloch & Wallis Ltd
25 Dering Street
London W1
01-629 0311

Manders Paint Ltd
P.O. Box 9
Mander House
Wolverhampton WV1 3NH
0902 711511

Martin-Thomas Ltd
South Way
Walworth Industrial Estate
Andover
Hampshire SP10 5AD
0264 4014

Megatron Ltd
165 Marlborough Road
London N19 4NE
01-272 3739

The Morden Company
7 Lytham Road
Heald Green
Cheadle
Cheshire SK8 3RO
061-437 4379

Nilfisk Ltd
Newmarket Road·
Bury St Edmunds
Suffolk IP33 3SR
0284 63163

Norfolk Industries for the Blind Ltd
95 Oak Street
Norwich
Norfolk NR3 3BP
0603 667957

Numatic International
Broadwindsor Road
Beaminster
Dorset DT8 3PR
0308 862062

A. S. Parker & Co. Ltd
45a Derby Road
Southport
Merseyside PR9 0TZ
0704 36404

Picreator Enterprises Ltd
44 Park View Gardens
Hendon
London NW4 2PN
01-202 8972

Quarry Bank Mill Trust Ltd
Styal
Wilmslow
Cheshire SK9 4LA
0625 527468

Raper & Sons Ltd
Chancellor Lane Industrial Estate
Handworth Street
Ardwick
Manchester M12 6LH
061-273 2524/5

Rentokil Ltd
Products Division
Felcourt
East Grinstead
West Sussex RH19 2JY
0342 833022

Roblin & Sons
112 High Street
Aylesbury
Buckinghamshire HP20 1RB
0296 23099

John Rusling Ltd
The Old Hall
Station Road
Newport
Shropshire TF10 7HU
0952 811779

Russell Scientific Instruments Ltd
Rashes Green Industrial Estate
Dereham
Norfolk NR19 IJG
0362 3481

G. Ryder & Co. Ltd
Denbigh Road
Bletchley
Milton Keynes
Buckinghamshire MK1 IDG
0908 75524

Secol Ltd
Kelvin Place
Thetford
Norfolk IP24 3RR
0842 2341

J. Shiner & Sons Ltd
8 Windmill Street
London W1P IHF
01-580 0740, 01-636 0740

James Smith & Son (Redditch) Ltd
Bromsgrove Road
Redditch
Worcestershire B97 4QY
0527 62034, 0527 68826

Solar X (UK) Ltd
Solar X House
8–12 Stockport Road
Cheadle Heath
Stockport
Cheshire SK3 0HZ
061-477 5040

Solvolene Lubricants Ltd
24 Reginald Square
London SE8 4RX
01-692 2241

Spicer Cowan Ltd
New Hythe House
Aylesford
Maidstone
Kent ME20 7PD
0622 77777
(Branches all over the UK – addresses in
Yellow Pages)

Tidmarsh & Sons
1 Laycock Street
London N1 1SW
01-226 2261

Transatlantic Plastics
Sales Office
23 Brighton Road
Surbiton
Surrey
01-339 5271

Ulster Weaving Co.
Linfield Industrial Estate
47 Linfield Road
Belfast BT12 5GL
0232 229494

Velcro Ltd
The Uplands
Biddulph
Stoke-on-Trent
Staffordshire ST8 7RH
0782 513316

A. Warne & Co. Ltd
41/43 Great Guildford Street
London SE1 0HB
01-261 1373

Waveney Apple Growers Ltd
Common Road
Aldeby
Beccles
Suffolk NR34 0BL
050277 345

Weetman & Co.
124 Ashley Road
Hale
Cheshire
061-928 0754

Wiggins Teape Paper Ltd
Gateway House
Basing View
Basingstoke
Hampshire RG21 2EE
0256 20262

Wilsons (Wearwell) Ltd (Mr Bryan)
Universal House
843-5 Green Lanes
Winchmore Hill
London N21 2RX
01-360 9366

J. Wippell & Co. Ltd
PO Box 1
88 Buller Road
St Thomas
Exeter EX4 1DQ
0392 54234

H. Wolfin & Son Ltd
64 Great Titchfield Street
London W1P 7AE
01-636 4949, 01-580 4724

PHOTOGRAPHIC
ACKNOWLEDGEMENTS

1. John Bethell; 2. John Bethell; 3. National Trust; 4. The Art Institute of Chicago; 5. John Bethell; 6. David Kilpatrick; 7. National Trust/Anthea Palmer; 8. Angelo Hornak; 9. Country Life/Alex Starkey; 10. Nicolette Hallett; 11. Jeremy Whitaker; 12. Judy Larney; 13. Judy Larney; 14. John Bethell; 15. A. C. Cooper; 16. Jonathan Betts; 17. Angelo Hornak; 18. National Trust; 19. Hawkley Studios; 20. National Trust; 21. John Bethell; 22. John Bethell; 23. John Bethell; 24. Angelo Hornak; 25. Angelo Hornak; 26. N. T. Waddesdon Manor; 27. N. T. Waddesdon Manor; 28. Jeremy Whitaker; 29. Jonathan Gibson; 30. A. C. Cooper; 31. Country Life; 32. Jeremy Whitaker; 33. John Bethell; 34. John Bethell; 35. John Bethell; 36. Molyneux Photography; 37. John Bethell; 38. John Bethell; 39. National Trust; 40. Fox Talbot Museum, Lacock; 41. Angelo Hornak; 42. Jonathan Gibson; 43. Jonathan Gibson; 44. Jonathan Gibson; 45. Hawkley Studios; 46. Angelo Hornak; 47. Jeremy Whitaker; 48. Angelo Hornak; 49. Angelo Hornak; 50. Angelo Hornak; 51. Paul Berkshire; 52. National Trust; 53. National Trust; 54. Angelo Hornak; 55. National Trust/Anthea Palmer; 56. National Trust/Anthea Palmer; 57. Molyneux Photography; 58. John Bethell; 59. National Trust; 60. John Bethell; 61. Sheila Stainton; 62. Yale Center for British Art, Paul Mellon Collection; 63. Angelo Hornak; 64. National Trust/Sheila Stainton; 65. Angelo Hornak; 66. John Bethell; 67. Jeremy Whitaker; 68. Nicolette Hallett; 69. Jeremy Whitaker; 70. John Bethell; 71. Angelo Hornak; 72. Molyneux Photography; 73. Angelo Hornak; 74. Angelo Hornak; 75. Country Life; 76. Country Life; 77. Molyneux Photography.

INDEX

Italic type indicates illustrations